PAULUS

PAULUS

REMINISCENCES
OF A FRIENDSHIP

ROLLO MAY

HARPER & ROW, PUBLISHERS
New York, Evanston, San Francisco, London

FIRST EDITION

Library of Congress Cataloging in Publication Data

May, Rollo.
  Paulus; a personal portrait of Paul Tillich.
  Includes bibliographical references.
  1. Tillich, Paul, 1886-1965. I. Title.
BX4827.T53M34   230'.092'4 [B]   72-78075
ISBN 0-06-065535-6

Contents

Preface

During the half-dozen years since the death of Paul Tillich, his widow, Hannah, has urged me to write a biography of him. I am grateful for her urging and for the aid she has given in this enterprise. As I reconsidered Paulus' fascinating life, however, I became convinced that the only area in which I could hope to do some justice was that in which our lives overlapped. Thus this book turns out to be about two men, Paulus and me, and how our lives intermingled from almost the month he stepped off the ship as an exile from Germany until his death in 1966. I have therefore subtitled it *Reminiscences of a Friendship*.

Rollo May
Holderness, New Hampshire

PAULUS

CHAPTER 1

Our First Meeting

I first met Paul Tillich in January of 1934. The encounter was anonymous for both of us. As I had come out of my room in Hastings Hall at Union Theological Seminary, I saw at the far end of the corridor a solitary man, hesitant and bewildered, making his way in my direction. Since it was the interim between semesters, all other students were gone; the hall was entirely empty and silent except for him and me.

The slanting rays of the winter sun shone through a glass door part way up the hall, and as he stopped in the sunlight I could see him more clearly. There was nothing in his medium height and nondescript gray suit that would have attracted any comment. But his countenance I still recall vividly today. A large leonine head with a shock of bushy hair over a high forehead. High color, and a face constructed not in curves but in planes, like a portrait by Cézanne. The horn-rimmed glasses added to his expression of hunting for something. I don't know how much of what I knew of him later I read back into the initial picture. But I do know that I was struck from the first by the chiseled character of his solid features; they seemed carved in marble, yet blended with a childlike winsomeness. My daughter, an artist, was visited in the hospital by Paulus (as he was called in his native German) when she was in her late teens, and often spoke afterward of his "beautiful head."

That day in January I helped him locate the room he was hunting for and then went on, closing the incident in my mind. Yet I could not forget that face.

In the previous August I had come back from three years in Greece, where I had been teaching at Anatolia College in Saloniki. There had been much time to travel in the vacations; I had spent two summers with a group of modern artists, painting and studying peasant art as we traveled. I had also attended, though briefly, seminars with Alfred Adler in Vienna. As a young man of twenty, I was impressed by the tragic sense of life which infused the culture of Europe, and especially that of ancient and modern Greece. It seemed to me that the delight in life and spontaneous joy which I had found a great deal more in Europe than in my years of growing up in Michigan had their source in depths which can be reached only by way of this tragic sense. Without it one experiences mere superficial amusement and comfort. Europe meant for me in those early thirties not only a physical emancipation but a new spiritual and intellectual freedom as well.

American psychology, to which I came back, seemed naïve and simplistic, omitting exactly what made life most rich and exciting. I longed for some community in which one could ask questions about the meaning of despair, suicide, and normal anxiety (a term never used in the American psychology of those days). If we posed these questions, we might also discover their counterparts: courage, joy, and intensity of living. Tocqueville was right, I believed, in thinking that while Americans are more physically free than their European cousins, they are more emotionally bound by conformism and more spiritually enslaved by fear of ostracism.

Not that I had ever had any inclination to live in Europe. I am American to the core, indeed middle western—in many ways the epitome of America. I knew American characteristics —such as generosity, friendliness, courage to risk and to experiment, energy—of which I was proud despite the fact that they go hand in hand with their opposites, such as violence and money-mindedness. The American character is complex indeed, and I wanted to throw in my lot with my countrymen. Loyalty to my country made all the stronger my hatred of our national violence and our spiritual vacuity. I had often read F. Scott Fitzgerald's statement on the last page of his incomparable novel on the American dream, *The Great Gatsby*, that the Dutch sailors who came here two centuries ago witnessed

the last and greatest of human dreams. . . . For a transitory enchanted moment man must have held his breath in the presence of this continent, compelled to an aesthetic contemplation he neither understood nor desired, face to face for the last time in history with something commensurate with his capacity for wonder.

I thought I partly understood that "contemplation" which made the sailors hold their breath in the presence of this continent. And I was sure I wanted to understand it more.

These are some of the reasons I found myself that winter in Union Theological Seminary. Though I abhorred many aspects of the organized Church, I had a passion for understanding life on a dimension that would be authentically human.

2

A week after our encounter in the hall I saw on the bulletin board a notice of a series of lectures to be given by a German scholar. His name meant nothing to me. But the titles! "The Spiritual Implications of Psychoanalysis," "The Religious Meaning of Modern Art"—and the same with Karl Marx and communism and other crucial aspects of our then-contemporary culture. At that time we were in a reaction against the bourgeoisie, and these lectures sounded like exactly the honest penetration into the problems of modern society for which I had hungered.

When I reached the classroom I saw on the platform my nameless acquaintance of the sunlit corridor. The class met on Friday afternoons, and there were only fifteen to twenty students plus half a dozen faculty members. One of the latter had been important in Tillich's coming to America: Reinhold Niebuhr.

Tillich sat at the lecture table, trying to pronounce his words in the English he was then just learning. Despite the broken language, I felt I had been waiting all my life for someone to speak out as he did. His words called forth truths in myself that I had known vaguely for years but never dared articulate. For example, that the best way to understand the spiritual temper of a historical period is to look at its art, since the artists of the time express the unconscious dimensions of the society. If one defines religion as Tillich did, as "ultimate concern," a picture by a modern artist which seems nihilistic and meaningless may well be more religious than a conventional painting of the head of Jesus by Hoffman. For another example: "God does not exist. He is not one being over against other beings, but being itself."

Tillich spoke with changing expressions of agony and joy reflecting in his face what was going on in his feeling at the moment. This gripped me with a sense of reality that I had never yet known in the intellectual world. No doubt it was also why Henry Sloane Coffin, then president of the seminary, who sat in on these first lectures, later remarked, "I don't understand what he says, but when I look at his face I believe."

Tillich treated questions with the greatest respect. When you asked something, no matter how insipid or inconsequential, he would assume you had some ultimate meaning in mind and would turn your question into one that made you proud, though you often did not understand either exactly what he was answering or what he said in his answer. He seemed to take for granted that all of us there—as Socrates says—would be at all times concerned with the ultimate questions of reason and love and death.

In one of those lectures Tillich said seriously, "If there is a devil I do not know." At this the class doubled up in laughter. It seemed funny in those days for someone to take the reality of the devil so solemnly. No doubt most of us did not pause to recall that this speaker had just come from his experience with Hitler.

Tillich's partial knowledge of English accounted in fact for a number of quite funny slips. He would speak of Beethoven's "Moonshine Sonata." In discussing some philosopher he would remark upon "spice and tame," and as the class burst into laughter corrected himself: "I always make that mistake—I mean 'tame and spice.' " To this day I cannot say "space and time" without remembering that contretemps.

Most of the students indeed were not used to hearing a German professor lecture, no matter how eminent. They roared with laughter, often at Tillich's mistakes and confusions in English. It served the purpose of relieving their tension in hearing such unusual lectures. One young man, I recall, put to him the question, "Didn't St. Paul get the world out of one mess to get it into another?" The reddish leonine face on the platform blushed a deeper red as Paulus looked pained and embarrassed and the class guffawed. He looked across at the door through which he had come, then his large head swung around toward the other side of the room, as though seeking the nearest exit for escape. Then he looked hopelessly at the class, "Vat iz 'mess'?" If he could scarcely as yet understand formal English, he was surely confused at the vernacular. Obligingly, the student rephrased the question, substituting "jam" for the offending word. And Tillich went through his whole charade again.

German professors are not used to being laughed at. I could see the pain behind the horn-rimmed glasses, and indeed the suffering on his face was a measure of the seriousness with which he took what he was saying. He often blushed, looking from face to face in the room as though somewhere there must be a resting place. Once he said to the class, "You laugh at my mistakes . . . ," like one trapped. Having just come from Europe, I knew how differently professors were treated there. I had signed more than one hotel register in Austria as required with the label of my profession, "Teacher," only to be greeted at the first meal by my name on the dining room place card preceded by "Herr Professor Doctor." It was disturbing to me to see Paulus' distress.

So I wrote him a short letter, which I put in his faculty mailbox. I tried to tell him that while the laughter might be *at* him it was not *against* him, and that his lectures were greatly valued by myself and the other students in the class. Aware that he did not know me from Adam, I thought it simply an anonymous gesture. At least it would allay my own discomfort when laughter arose again. It is, I think, one of the inheritances of the American which is not found in Europe, where everyone minds his own business, that if you happen upon someone needing help you give it, whether the person is stranger, foreigner, or friend.

But Paulus somehow discovered my identity and came up to me in the hall a week later; he said that my letter had been very important for him. In thanking me he explained as best he could—still preserving the typically German barrier against premature intimacy—how it had helped him through a critical period.

In the late spring of that year I heard that my mother and father were being divorced. With a sense of duty which I later realized in psychoanalysis was much too Oedipal, I abandoned my studies for the time being and went to East Lansing to take care of what was left of the family—my mother and younger sister and brother. I got a job at Michigan State College and remained there for two years. I heard rumors of Tillich from time to time, especially when I went down to Chicago, for he was by then teaching at the university there. One heard what a remarkable scholar and philosopher he was, and how the faculty venerated him.

When I came back to New York, Tillich had also returned. He had learned to laugh good-naturedly along with the students at his mistakes. How much he really felt like laughing and how much it was an adaptation technique I do not know. But it worked. As a teacher he was now arrivé. His classes overflowed, and he had become what many persons who studied with him in New York or Chicago or Harvard were later to call the most creative teacher they ever had.

3

Later, when Paulus and I became friends, I was to learn that he had grown up in a small, rustic walled town in eastern Germany where his father had been the Lutheran minister. Herds of cattle and sheep were driven through the streets morning and evening. His boyhood was spent in company not only with these ever-present animals and the village children but also in close communion with the change of seasons reflected in the silent plowlands round about. The town was protective and sheltering, and its vitality and animation at night against the weird, dark forest surrounding its clustered fields made a lasting impression on him.

Most important of all, its civic rights and tradition went back to the Middle Ages. Paulus himself says that the eastern part of Germany was never fully Christianized; the old legends still held their power. Every stone in the walls, as well as the ancient town gates, spoke out of centuries of myth, ritual, and folklore. Many of us in America have grown up in drab, jerry-built towns developed on principles of conspicuous consumption, and

Henry Ford could plaster placards all over the country proclaiming "History Is Bunk" because it was our conventional
faith that history began at the last board meeting. We had to
garner our beauty outside the towns in the woods and rivers
and mountains of America. But in his town Paulus was surrounded by the very presence of the poetry and legends he
studied in school. To grow up in towns in which "every stone
is witness of a period many centuries past," Paulus was later to
write, "produces a feeling for history . . . as a living reality in
which the past participates in the present." [1] The very air and
soil around him were animated, and they fed his already lively
imagination.

We students knew that Tillich was an emigré from Hitler's
Germany and that he had the honor of being the first Christian
to be dismissed from his university professorship when Hitler
came to power. But no one knew the details. I later pieced
together, mostly from incidents told me by Paulus and his wife
Hannah, the story of the Götterdämmerung of those last
months.

The Germany of the Weimar Republic had been marked by
increasing despair. The war-guilt clause from World War I still
hung like a millstone around every German's neck. The lower
middle class was being progressively squeezed out, and a kind
of spiritual deterioration, accompanied by a disintegration of
values and goals, took hold of the people. On one hand the arts
flourished, as seen in the expressionistic painting of that time
and the original products of the Bauhaus School. But Paulus told
how the middle classes mocked this art; he could not go to
exhibitions during those years without being beset by Germans
who leered at the pictures as if at display of pornography.

A *fin de siècle* mood prevailed. Sexual mores were in radical

---

1. *The Theology of Paul Tillich,* paperback, ed. by Charles W. Kegley and
R.   W. Bretall (New York: The Macmillan Company, 1961), p. 5.

disruption, and a decadent air surrounded the new sensuality.

In such a milieu Hitlerism or something like it was bound to emerge. Paulus and his colleagues tried to stem the tide; they would go to east Berlin and make speeches to the workers about religious socialism. But the next night the Nazis would come and from the same platform twist their words into other meanings, capitalizing on what Paulus and his colleagues had said to gain support for National Socialism. Paulus could hold his own in any kind of open debate—that one as well; by some confusion in both our minds about what the audience was to be, I took him, back in 1937 or 1938, to a meeting of young Communists in New York City. When they attacked him, he deftly turned their arguments against themselves. To the accusation, "You are only proclaiming an ideology," he responded, "You say every other idea is an ideology except communism. That is not a very consistent theory to say the least!" But the situation in this country was very different from Germany in the early thirties. Tillich felt the helplessness of his or anyone else's ability to hold back the flood. It was clear that he and the fatherland no longer spoke or understood the same language.

One of his students was beaten up outside the classroom by Nazi hoodlums. Paulus helped carry him into the building. In his lectures he then shifted to a denunciation of the Nazis in as strong words as he could find. He and Hannah went to hear Hitler in person, and through an industrialist they were able to get seats on the speakers' platform. But after the speech both were sick and in despair; this was a barbarian, Paulus moaned, who could not even use the German language.

The German Church officially began to bend toward Hitler, which increased his feeling of desperation. In the book-burning episodes they witnessed, the number of books destroyed was not great but the symbol was horrifying. Paulus became enraged at this maniacal behavior. As I knew him, he was almost anger-proof: I saw him angry only twice in the whole thirty-odd years of our friendship. But in those days he seemed to be in a continuous rage, the more so as the time of fatal decision approached.

The story then becomes one of clandestine interviews and long secret meetings after dark; Berlin seemed like a city under siege. Paulus volunteered to write for the underground press. But others thought his style was too easily recognizable; it would be dangerous for them. One had to be careful with every sentence uttered to one's hairdresser, lest it be blurted out to the storm troopers next day.

Paulus took Hitler as a catastrophe of barbarism, but people outside Germany could not really believe that things were really as reported. Europe that summer was filled with jokes about Adolph the First, a handy device for not taking the coming catastrophe seriously. In my three years in Europe I had never visited Germany—perhaps because of a certain premonition of what was to happen. But in August 1933 I did take a train, with a Viennese artist friend, from Vienna to Bremen, from which our boat was to sail. We entrained at night, and when I woke in the morning I commented to my traveling companion that I was surprised to see that this was Germany, for there was grass growing, and I had expected to see the hills sprouting knives. He immediately edged me down the car to the men's washroom, and in this one available private place gave me strict orders not to say anything like that again in Germany.

In the cities of Germany itself the mood grew more frivolous as it became more despairing. Parties were held on all sides, and people kissed as though it were the last time they would ever have the chance—which in some instances was in fact the case. Several gatherings to which Hannah and Paulus were invited were followed the next night by the suicide of the host and hostess. Suicide was in the air; it was a reality on all sides.

During that summer of 1933 Tillich received long-distance

phone calls from Horace Friess, head of the department of philosophy at Columbia University, then in Italy, and Reinhold Niebuhr in New York. Both urged him to come to lecture at Columbia and Union Seminary. But Paulus had always felt that to leave Germany was to desert the intellectual capital of the world—one of the few arrogances he permitted himself.

He was also resolved not to leave voluntarily. He made an appointment with the Secretary of Education, a government appointee and took Hannah with him to Berlin for the conference. She waited in the café downstairs as the men talked earnestly for over an hour. Taking the initiative in the conversation from the first, Paulus raised two questions on which he demanded answers, which would be decisive for his own position. Was the government going to continue the persecution of the Jews? And what was to be the policy toward modern culture? Finally the Secretary, seeing him adamant, advised him to leave the country for at least two years.

Paulus arrived back at the café table and threw down before Hannah three steamship tickets to America, for her, their daughter, and himself. He had bought them on the way down from the Secretary's office.

In a burst of generosity, Hannah seized her purse and ran down to a taxi driver sitting in his car.

"Do you have any children?" she cried.

When he nodded, she grabbed the bills in her purse and stuffed them in his hand. "Buy them something with this! My husband's life has just been saved."

CHAPTER 2

Ecstatic Reason

The term "ecstatic reason" is one Tillich used, and for me it most accurately describes his thinking. The brilliance and profundity of his mind, after all, is the essential reason he stands in the line of those great figures who have moved the world with the word rather than the sword. I might have entitled this chapter "Transcendent Reason," since both terms refer to reason going beyond mere intellectualizing—reason caught up by "ultimate concern" and therefore embracing values and poetry and justice. "Ecstatic reason is reason grasped by ultimate concern," Paulus wrote. "Reason is overpowered, invaded, shaken by the ultimate concern."[1] Ecstatic or transcendent reason is that of the thinker who, like Plato, has the courage to leap into the realm of mythology when the truth he wishes to express requires it.

Paulus knew that transcendent reason had fallen on hard times in our day. Dominant at the time of Spinoza, it had now become largely "technical reason," that is, reason devoted to calculations, a kibbitzing on science. He also knew that the reaction against technical reason would occur in America as it already had in his native Germany, i.e., in the destructive

1. *Systematic Theology* (Chicago: University of Chicago Press, 1951), 1:53.

romanticism of the Hitler movement. This reaction against dry, dead intellectualizing has indeed taken place in this country, on one hand in the form of anti-intellectualism and the devotion to feeling-touching, and on the other in the worship of "pseudo-scientific techniques" of selecting a new personality every weekend.

My own childhood in Michigan had given me a sufficient dose of anti-intellectualism. I grew up close to the frontier, where it made sense to be afraid of "thinking too much." A sympathetic man in other respects, my father regularly remarked that the trouble with my older sister, who had gone through a psychotic breakdown, was that she "had too much education." I sensed how inhuman and destructive this remark was, but there were no other persons around who did not speak the same language. I could not help being to some extent maimed by the disease of anti-intellectualism and I hated it.

At college there was an ancient Greek vase on the table in the seminar room where our class in Greek was held. Fresh from Michigan, I had never seen anything before with lines so simple and yet so beautiful, and I marveled at it day after day. In those hours of a student's trancelike wonder there was born the resolve, unconscious at first, to go to Greece. When I did arrive in Athens two years later, there began my love affair with the indomitable spirit of the ancient Greeks. This was partly romantic but in part entirely reasonable. I had a passionate need to live, at least inwardly, in the world of Plato, Socrates, and Euripides—a spiritual realm that seemed much more real to me than the neon-lighted city of Detroit, or the inevitably drab Main Streets of middle America, or the limitations of mind that led to my father's cruel remark.

I brought this spirit of ancient Greece back with me. And the important point is that I immediately identified Tillich with it. His profound respect for the human mind was for me an oasis in a desert. Yet his reason could soar—hence the terms transcendent and ecstatic. He had also a concept of logos which was the basis of his overwhelming power of logic—not in the cheap sense of beating down an opponent in debate (which he could do but in fact rarely did, for the practice leaves everyone a little emptier than before no matter who gains the logical victory). His deep sense of logic was rather a relation to the cosmos: the belief that everything that exists is related in profound dimensions to everything else. With Paulus as my teacher I found I no longer needed to keep my spiritual self underground.

I sensed a direct line from the eminent figures of ancient Greece—Aeschylus, Sophocles, Phidias—down to Paulus himself.[2] Each seemed to me intensely vital; each lived with a seriousness that was not sober; each knew that death would come sooner or later and that there was therefore no time for prevarication or dishonesty with oneself. Each burned with the gemlike flame that comes from the knowledge that we are on this crust of earth for our little moment to build our machines or think and speak our thoughts or sing our poems. Aeschylus put together his magnificent dramas, Phidias constructed a Parthenon, and Paulus took all knowledge, Faust-like, as his province, and through knowing constructed a system of thought which has at once beauty, symmetry, and convincing power. I saw these men as living not by some new technique found in the laboratory yesterday, nor by some new truth discovered in an oriental shrine two days ago. Rather they believed this was the way life was if, to quote Matthew Arnold on Sophocles, you "saw life steadily and saw it whole."

I was partly wrong, of course. In the content of his thought, Paulus is closer to the archaic Greek philosophers, such as Hera-

2. In describing his education, Paulus was later to state his debt to the spirit of ancient Greece. "My love of the Greek language was a vehicle for my love of the Greek culture and especially the early Greek philosophers." *The Theology of Paul Tillich*, paperback, ed. by Charles W. Kegley and Robert W. Bretall (New York: The Macmillan Company, 1961), p. 9.

clitus, Empedocles, and Parmenides, than to those of the classical age. But I was right in connecting his symphonic way of thinking with the "circle" culture of ancient Greece. In Paulus' thinking everything comes back, from the depths of the abyss as well as the heights of ecstasy, to fit everything else. It gave me an experience of revelation similar to that when I saw the Greek shoreline and rounded hills rising to meet the curves of the Parthenon and coming back again to become part of the curving shoreline and the sea.

I had had brilliant professors or colorful ones or ones who cared about communicating knowledge or were profound in their reflection on the human predicament. But I had never had one who brought all these things together. Three words summarize Paulus' lectures for me: universality, depth, and caring. The main thing was, whatever he was discussing, *it mattered.* Nietzsche's aphorism, "All truths are bloody truths to me," became real in Tillich's lectures. In my solitary walks in Riverside Park after his class to let the ideas sink in, I was filled with a profound seriousness and joy, not only about the truths I had heard but also about my own life and the decisions I had to make. This same combination of joy and seriousness was, I believed, what gave dignity to the sculptures in ancient Greece which I had gone back to look at again and again, always with a new sense of wonder.

The same charismatic quality had been present in Paul Tillich from the beginning of his teaching. Hannah gives her impression of an early lecture of his when he was sought after by the intellectual circles of Berlin.[3] He was

a youthful looking man with a bush of blonde hair, very strong eyeglasses which he had to wear for reading and distance, shabbily dressed, shy in person. I remember seeing him before he gave the lecture at the Kant institute which made him famous; he walked

3. From notes sent to me by Hannah Tillich several years ago.

around before the lecture, greeting friends here and there, talking, asking questions, giving an impression of clumsiness and uncertainty about what to say. I watched him and I thought, Oh, my God!

But when he entered the speaker's podium he had an intensive emanation, a transformation from the very first words. Indecision had gone, the voice was clear and powerful, he became the instrument of his thinking power; he was only the *logos* and whatever he said had conviction, aroused your own thinking power. It was a magnificent display of a new world vision, and the past and future and present were called up to give the foundation for it. He was in no way a superficial visionary, he had done impressive philosophical and theological reading; but more than that he had entered into the spirit of his books, he knew the material and he could make you see it from a new angle. In discussion he listened and showed an understanding of the question, then went on to fill it with new significance and interest. He took all the arguments into his vision and elaborated them in such a way that he seemed all-embracing in spirit and intellect. The audience felt new ways opened up of world and self-understanding.

The all-embracing quality of Paulus' thinking amazed me in his first lectures and has continued to amaze me ever since. After the death of Alfred North Whitehead, who had a similar breadth, there was no one I knew in America who had such scope and the vast knowledge to make it real. Horace Friess at Columbia has remarked that graduate students in philosophy had a tendency to imitate Tillich in their penchant for making generalizations about history. The trouble was, he continued, they lacked Tillich's vast and comprehensive knowledge of history, which is necessary if such insights are to be convincing.

Once I introduced him at a lecture as follows:

Paul Tillich's thought reminds me of an experience I have had several times standing on the top of Mt. Washington in New Hampshire. From that highest mountain in New England you can see off to the west the state of Vermont, to the south the range of the other White Mountains, to the southeast the Atlantic ocean, to the east Maine, and to the north

Canada. Tillich's mind has the same vastness: you feel the spirit of the ancient Greeks, the Middle Ages, the Renaissance, and the modern age all brought together in one all-embracing, harmonious whole.

But often when I stand on Mt. Washington the fog comes down and the mists envelop me so that I can barely see my hand in front of my face. Yet at those moments I know that the states of Vermont and Maine and the Atlantic Ocean and Canada are still there whether I can see them or not. Sometimes the mist descends and gives me the same feeling when listening to Paul Tillich's speeches. But no matter how fog-bound my own mind may be, I still know that the ages and cultures are alive in Tillich's mind even though *I* cannot see them. I am reassured by the awareness that sooner or later the fog of my own obtuseness will be blown away.

The audience laughed with recognition, for they too had experienced the same great vistas of thought in Tillich which at times left us all far behind.

Contrary to a widespread misunderstanding, ecstatic reason does not come by cultivating the "ecstasy" without the "reason." Along with Tillich's erudition, it was the result of long, disciplined study interspersed with periods of solitude. When Hannah used to come to see him in his early thirties in his Berlin apartment before their marriage, he would put her to bed late in the evening and then go up to his study to work most of the rest of the night. In a letter to a friend thanking her for sending a picture of St. Anthony meeting temptation in the desert, Paulus wrote, "It was in 1919 in Berlin, when I withdrew from all social obligations in order to do my scientific work, that my friend and brother-in-law sent the Grünewald picture of St. Anthony with nice, joking verses. At that time I did not succumb."

In New York and East Hampton he had a similar working schedule of two or three hours in the morning, generally lectures in the afternoon, then dinner with family or friends. Then came the most prized time of all, from ten or eleven till one in the morning, working in the perfect solitude of night.

2

Tillich had begun his philosophical career as a German ideal-
ist, trained as he was in classical thought. He believed in the
identity of essence and existence—that man could master the
essence of his being by cognitive means. But one night, while
he was a chaplain in World War I, in a battle on the Marne all
that changed. His fellow officers were brought in on stretchers,
chopped to pieces by gunfire, wounded or dead. That night
"absolutely transformed me," he used to say. "All my friends
were among these dying and dead. That night I became an
existentialist." From then on he could no longer separate truth
from the human being who acts on it; right and wrong were no
longer decided purely at ethereal heights of thought; the living,
pulsing, committing, suffering and loving human being must
always be taken into account. With new insight he then read
Nietzsche, an "ecstatic experience in the fields and forests, in
my times off from the war duties."

Paulus' thought always demands of readers or listeners not
ivory-towered agreement but decisions and risk. The dynamic
basis of this is a simple question, the question with which all
metaphysics begins. He once told us in a class discussion of his
great sense of shock when, early in his career, he asked himself
this question: "Why is there *something?* Why not *nothing?*" It
had come to him as he read it in Lessing, and it disturbed him
profoundly. If you take this question seriously you are pushed
to the very roots of existence. The question calls for reflection
in the ultimate sense; to ask it is to find yourself at the basis of
being. If there were not something, no one would be here even
to *know* there was nothing. It is the human mind's "to be or not
to be" in the ultimate sense. No one, obviously, can answer it
definitively; yet this question must underlie all philosophy
worthy of the name. Those who are immediately tempted to

give a scientific answer do not understand the question itself. It is not an objective query, nor is it a subjective one; it must be asked on the level that underlies the split between objectivity and subjectivity.

Paulus knew it for a question which must be lived out rather than thought out. This gave an intuitive, penetrating quality to his lectures. When he talked about the most universal concept of all—namely, being—you felt it was no empty word. Nor did you have to translate it into the German *Sein* to give it meaning. You felt *your* being made alive, at hand, as close as your heartbeat. It was your destiny made immediately accessible to your understanding and experience.

This question—Why is there something and not nothing?—has a similar startling effect upon me whenever I ask it of myself. It makes me grateful for being, grateful that there *is* being, that I can be aware of others' being and can experience my own. But it also means that every truth must be wedded to its action. Pure abstract thinking (if it were possible—which it is not) would be immoral, and pure action without thought (if that were possible—which again it is not) would be a betrayal of the self.

Tillich's dialectical skill was so great and his knowledge of the various philosophies so comprehensive that he seemed never at a loss in disputation. He argued from *within* each system, often understanding its meaning better than those defending it. Once in a discussion with Herbert Schneider, professor of philosophy at Columbia and a Spinozistic determinist, after a few moments Paulus smiled with an openhanded gesture and said simply, "If you are determined to be a determinist . . ." The double meaning of that comment covers the argument better than a week of talk.

He had the rare capacity of being an authority without being authoritarian. One night in 1937 I took him up to speak to a small group of students at New York University, to whom I was advisor. Tillich discussed with them his conviction that the age we live in was one of dissolution and that the Western world was on the brink of cataclysm. It was the theme which some of us later affectionately dubbed the "ruins-ruins-ruins" motif. That evening he approached it on the basis of his vast knowledge of history and the cycles of rise and fall of nations. The students as usual were deeply impressed; but they did not know how to take such dire predictions, living as they did in the falsely optimistic period of the middle thirties. As we walked home I told Paulus how much I valued the discussion. Then I added, "But I cannot believe you."

He stopped in the street and turned to me, "You must not believe me." I was young, he said, and I must have hope in order to work for what I believed. His implication, as I see it now, was that each one of us must live out the stage in which he is at the given moment. Probably he had a pretty good idea that in due course I would experience enough of the world to come to my own conclusions, and that they would be fairly similar to his. This is what indeed happened. But his concern for me that evening, a concern superseding what was abstractly "true" and "false," I have always greatly appreciated.

Paulus believed strongly in the value as well as the pleasure, at times even ecstasy, of sheer thinking. He quoted Aristotle with agreement, "Pure theory gives pure eudaimonia." On one occasion, when he and some students were trying to arrange a time to meet for a discussion, they pointed out, still under the illusion that education consists of memorizing facts, that the examination period began the next day. Paulus remarked, "The best preparation for an exam is a couple of hours of intense thinking the night before." He meant this *not* as thinking about the subject matter of the exam, but as sheer thinking.

I experienced a strange demonstration of this fact. At the beginning of my senior year at Union Seminary, I was invited by a publisher to write a book based on some lectures I had given the previous summer.[4] After some consideration I decided I would do it. The decision made it necessary to cut all my classes at the seminary (except Tillich's, which I would not have considered missing under any circumstances). For exams, I was concerned only to pass. I would rely simply on reading the text the day and night before the exam—a new form of truancy for me. At the end of the year, to my great surprise, I found myself graduating *cum laude,* chiefly on the basis of the excellent grades I received for *that year.* I expressed my astonishment to Paulus. He was not surprised in the least. "When you become creative in any field," he stated, "your creativity is released in all other fields at the same time." A new idea to me, but one that worked then and has done so a number of times since.

3

Three years after my graduation I was back at Columbia University studying for my doctorate in clinical psychology. My Ph.D. thesis was on theories of anxiety, later to be published as *The Meaning of Anxiety.* Paulus was one of my advisors, the one who directed me for those years most arduously and with most concern.

"You must know *everything* about anxiety," he insisted. "Everything ever written, thought, every research up to this day." I remonstrated. Nobody I knew had ever known everything about anything. But he quietly and firmly insisted. He believed that if you know one thing completely, it serves as a center—like a magnet around which iron filings coalesce—for all your other knowledge. Then what you learn about anything else will fall into pattern.

Nine difficult years of reading, thinking, research, and writing

4. This, my first book, written when I was twenty-seven, was published under the title *The Art of Counseling* (Nashville: Abingdon-Cokesbury, 1938). It was much influenced by my contact with Alfred Adler during the summers I was in Europe.

went into that book. Filled as I was with my new knowledge, I would sometimes write chapters bursting with arrogant generalizations (not untypical of Ph.D. candidates). With a patience the persistence of which I now look back on with wonder and gratitude, Paulus would calmly point out my errors of detail. Smarting under his criticism and his heavy requirements, I would accuse him of expecting an impossible perfection, or of expressing his own sadism with me as the victim. He would smile barely perceptibly, but still insist. He would accept nothing short of my knowing everything there was to know about anxiety.

Years later as I traveled to universities and colleges, psychologists and philosophers would tell me that at some time or other they had had lunch—let us say—with Tillich, and he had talked about this book with obvious pride. This gave me feelings of deepest pleasure, and I was also flattered. When I am told that the book is recognized as the first to effect a genuine union of psychology and philosophy, and also the first to demonstrate the importance of values for psychology, I recall with grateful humor all the struggles I had with Paulus. Once in a great while it may be a good thing to have someone expect perfection of you!

A great teacher, like a good therapist, changes with his students. In the arduous years while Paulus directed me in the meaning of anxiety, he thought a good deal about how people *confront* anxiety. We had together established the concept of normal anxiety; but this still leaves the question, when a person recognizes his *Angst,* how does he or she meet it? Out of this questioning came Paulus' Terry lectures given at Yale University in 1950, later to be published as *The Courage to Be.*

It is not at all surprising that Paulus should write on the subject of courage. He was morally courageous to an unusual degree in his stand against Hitler, in his continuous existence on intellectual frontiers, and even in his erotic life. He believed

that the problem of God is itself actually the problem of courage. Courage is taken in that book not as a virtue alone but as
both ethical *and* ontological. It is the courage of the human
being who is aware of his being and takes the responsibility for
affirming and actualizing it. But for me the book—possibly the
most significant introduction to his thought and certainly the
most widely read of his writings—will always be a token of the
interrelationship, dialectic if you will, between Paulus and myself. He has said from time to time that *The Courage to Be* was
written as an answer to *The Meaning of Anxiety,* a statement
which honors me more than I can say.

Some years later a birthday party was given for me, marking
the half-century point of my life. At the party Paulus made a
short speech. In typical German fashion, he recounted my career, ending with the statement that the thing that impressed
him above all was my struggle against tuberculosis. The guests
demanded a reply. As I got to my feet I had a strange thought.
After expressing deep appreciation to Paulus for all I had
learned from him and all he had meant to me as a friend,
mentor, and spiritual father, I said I had often wondered how
I would have turned out if I had never met Paulus. And I found
myself saying that I thought I would have turned out about the
same.

This statement greatly surprised even me. But that evening
Hannah was nodding her head vociferously, and Paulus also
nodded a quieter agreement. What I meant was that a person
finds the human beings he needs to guide him, to influence
him. The Greek concept of entelechy has always impressed me:
that the ultimate form is contained in the seed, and the tree or
animal or human being grows toward this form, malformed
though he may be in the process. I have seen trees in New
Hampshire growing around big rocks, fastening their roots to
the rock as they grow, or pushing through crevasses or clinging
to steep river banks where I was surprised that anything could

live. But they still grow upward, putting out their branches in precisely the direction needed for balance. Different as man is from a tree, he still has the vitality that pushes him toward what he needs to become, despite a disturbed childhood or chronic depression or a bad marriage or critical illnesses. With all our knowledge of the importance of environment, I do not see how we can escape some Tolstoyan belief, as a counterweight to influences from the outside, in the significance of the individual in history. And though I shiver to think what would have become of me if I had not known Tillich, I believe I would have struggled on to find in someone or several others my teachers and my guidance.

I felt a surge of love for Paulus that evening for recognizing this in his nodding, and for seeing that it did not detract in the slightest from my gratitude toward him: teacher and friend who gave me more than all other teachers I ever had combined.

CHAPTER 3

Paulus'
Personal Presence

At dinner at the home of a poet I happened to mention that I was writing a short biography of Tillich. There was a momentary hush over the small group at the table and a meditative look in their eyes as each remembered the time he or she had seen Tillich or heard him speak or talked with him. "Oh, Paul Tillich," someone murmured, "a remarkable man," and others dropped some comment about his impact upon them. During this pause I was struck, as I have been countless times before, by the quality of Paulus' presence with persons like these.

For the most frequently mentioned characteristic of Paulus is his presence. This was surely true of his lectures. It was well illustrated once at Dartmouth College, where I had gone the week before to give a speech in their Great Issues series. The Dartmouth committee had frankly written that they wanted me to provide a kind of bridge for the students to Paulus' thought—a John-the-Baptist role which I readily accepted. At lunch with a group of professors, the talk drifted to the sources of Tillich's great influence on students. One of them remarked that it was because of his "stage presence." I must have looked quizzical at this, for he hastened to add that he was referring to how Tillich's face changed expression with everything he said—showing sometimes agony, sometimes wonder, sometimes joy, but in any case mirroring his inner, personal commitment to what he was saying. When Rudolf Serkin plays the piano, the emotions of the music can be seen in his facial contortions; this was how it was with Tillich. The muscles of his face reflected his idea just before he uttered it in words; he seemed to live through the meaning of what he was saying right there on the stage.

The truth is, Paulus lived with his emotions always showing. In a poker game he would have been thoroughly fleeced. In the midst of our culture, where it is considered demeaning to wear your heart on your sleeve, in the good as well as bad sense, Paulus could not help doing so. I had never realized before how much a face could change. One could read the altering of his thoughts through his bodily expression, from serious peering through his horned-rimmed glasses to a momentary agonizing when he did not understand a word in a question someone asked, to pacing up and down the room, hands locked behind him, when he was in deep thought.

When he lectured, each person in the audience felt that Tillich was addressing him directly and individually, no matter how huge the gathering might be. This had to do with his smile —unflinchingly childlike, with no aggressiveness whatever, it was an endearing and uniquely personal smile. Paulus could be intellectually aggressive when he wished to be: when students talked in an undertone in class he would peer at them with, as he put it, "aggressivity." Otherwise his smile wouldn't have been so powerful. It reached out and invited you; it put you immediately on his side.

He had the quality of great actors that when he was on-stage attention was completely fixed upon him. Actors can explain this no more than anyone else: when I have questioned some of them about it they mention concentration, intensity of feeling, and other things, but end up with the statement that "presence" remains undefinable. Even Goethe, who related it to his view of the daimonic, considered it ultimately a mystery. But while personal presence will always have an elusive element, we must try to understand it as far as we can.

Tillich's own experience in such lectures is shown in a comment in his "Autobiographical Reflections":

I have always walked up to a desk or pulpit with fear and trembling, but the contact with the audience gives me a pervasive sense of joy, the joy of a creative communion, of giving and taking, even if the audience itself is not vocal.[1]

The way he handled questions from the audience after a lecture shows another aspect of this same quality of presence. Not understanding much of what had been said, many a person would ask a question which initially struck others as silly. I have already noted how Paulus would consider the question, find some deeper meaning in it, rephrase it, and answer it in light of the meaning he had himself revealed. The puzzled inquirer would be honored at such brilliance, even though he did not by then quite grasp either the question *or* the answer. This could border on the ungenuine, yet I never knew Paulus not to state it in a form that was truly interesting to him, which invariably meant to the rest of us. He was always on the alert for something he could learn—he often asked us students our opinion on a word: could "spirit" be used? he would ask. And what were the different meanings of "spiritual"?

Tillich's genius for presence was especially apparent in his personal relationships. Once during my second year at the seminary, when I did not yet know him except as my professor, I happened to be coming down the Broadway hill beside the Columbia campus and saw him walking up the west side of the

1. In *The Theology of Paul Tillich*, paperback, ed. by Charles W. Kegley and Robert W. Bretall (New York: The Macmillan Company, 1961), p. 15.

street. It was autumn. He was without the beret he generally wore in lieu of a hat, coatless, his gray jacket blowing in the wind. He gestured to me, so I crossed the street. As we met he immediately began, "What you said at the student meeting yesterday was very important. You were rightly cautious. Now tell me what you *really* think." He took my arm and turned me around so that I would accompany him a little way toward the subway station. And for the next five minutes we were deep into an interesting conversation.

What transpired in this brief episode? I felt much gratified that he had so clearly listened to what I said at the meeting; obviously I was slightly flattered. His phrase, "you were rightly cautious," is reassuring, and tells me he allies himself with me, takes the topic from my viewpoint. This identification with the other person is essential in "presence." It was a corollary in Paulus of his penchant for counting himself in on all human frailties. Even his slight I-won't-take-no-for-an-answer in taking hold of my arm and making me turn to fall in step with him shows how immediately he established a basis of intimacy. None of this was subterfuge: when he asked, he really did want to know.

But most important was the intensity of his concentration on whoever was with him. I felt absorbed, caught up, completely grasped by the experience. Everyone who knew him remarked on his capacity to attend completely to the other person. It gave one the pleasant sensation of *being known* (here the trite phrase does have a specific meaning) better, for that moment, than one knew oneself. I refer here to the degree of emotional and psychological nakedness that one experienced with Paulus, the refreshing feeling of touching a new level of honesty. It is a pleasure to be known, listened to, and have one's opinion authentically asked for and valued. A conversation with Paulus opened up qualities in you which you did not know were there, and after talking with him you went away with a new part of your self discovered.

It was eros that informed his intense presence in his relations with women. This was the source of his capacity to penetrate the woman with his eyes and voice, to a depth below that in which she had always looked at herself. His valuing of her opened up new possibilities which she had not known before. There was nothing mundane or boring around Paulus!

The presence of Paulus regularly brought a kind of joy, a mild ecstasy. The sexual analogy is not out of place: it was an experience of being psychologically and spiritually penetrated, it was exciting, and you felt new sensations. Obviously there was a good deal of libido in this presence, especially felt by women, and it partly accounts for their feeling of elation when he was around. But the pleasure of his presence was as common for men, though differently experienced.

2

Paulus believed that every encounter with a new person is anxiety-creating. Anxiety is present in every authentic encounter, that is, one in which people let themselves genuinely meet. This anxiety is the dread of freedom; in Kierkegaard's words, it is the "dizziness of freedom." You don't know what is ahead or what demands the encounter may make upon you, or the possibilities in this new relationship. You know you must risk something in order to go through with it, but you don't know how much. Also the pleasures, delights, and joys it can give you are still unknown. The meeting may jar you off your present course. It may bring a new expansion in your life or it may push you toward curtailment and psychological slavery.

We instinctively know this in the faster heartbeat and tremors we feel at moments of meeting a new person. We are only aware that something will be given to us and something demanded; we know we cannot stay in the same rut—something new is required.

I have been speaking of *new* relationships. But the same

anxiety-creating element appears, generally with less intensity, in any relationship in which new possibilities are uncovered. It occurs, for example, between spouses in enlightened marriages, where couples go through cycles of new discovery of themselves and their partners. And it certainly occurs with old friends, again generally on a less intensive scale.

The instinctive reaction is to protect oneself until the coast is clear, to hide one's own originality, one's impulses and native responses. The mechanics for doing this lie in the standards of courtesy, good manners, and so on, under whose aegis we conceal our authentic selves. But we do it at the price of falsifying ourselves. No matter how "necessary" such protection is, or the fact that no one could survive without such social forms, it is still very important that this protecting of oneself be done consciously. If you repress and do not know you are repressing, there is a danger of suffocation, a stultifying of the self. The problem of honesty in personality relationships is difficult indeed.

One of Paulus' refreshing traits was that he never tried to hide his embarrassment or blushing or discomfort, when these occurred. This was a matter of continual surprise to me. I was accustomed to eminent persons, and especially professors, covering up their intimate emotions. As a student I saw Paulus in many meetings of groups of people, blushing or looking in despair or pacing up and down the hall during a recess in the discussion. And I wondered why he did not control his emotions more effectively. But I later learned that the more one covers them up, the more distant and unavailable they become, the end result of which is the deadness and artificiality of obsessive and compulsive personality types. How I came to appreciate the courageous way Paulus went directly into meetings, alike with princes or paupers, never letting the fact that he was embarrassed or uncomfortable inhibit what he had to say and to give!

I used to notice at times how intently he looked at me or at others. It was an X-ray look, as though he were searching me out—for what? Neither condemning nor approving, he just looked at me as though he realized there were parts of me which he did not yet know. Was this an awareness in him of the variety and multiplicity of encounter with another person? Was he wondering about, or searching out, possibilities not yet expressed, or perhaps even known to *me*? When his logic did not intrude, he seemed to live out a vast spectrum of nuances in encounter with other human beings.

The mystery lies in the fact that one has two unknowns meeting each other. I do not fully know myself, in the sense that there are possibilities in me which are unactualized; they are like unexplored tracts of life I carry with me—to my surprise, sometimes, at what comes out. The other person is obviously unknown. We cannot expect him to stand still while we learn to know him, like a horse at auction; he will be changing even during our encounter with him. Such is the richness of human consciousness. If he is a stranger, he is very much unknown; even an old friend is still partly so. Each new meeting has its possibilities of surprise. This is kept to a minimum by conventions and accepted standards of decorum; but these accomplish what they are purposed to do only at the price of blocking off the new, the surprising, the shocking. This is why too great a reliance on codes of behavior and courtesy can result in the deadening of experience, the flattening out of relationship. Shyness is an expression of the inner experience of these risks; shy people may have a great deal to give in a relationship, and their shyness may mean simply a sensing of their own possibilities.

But what about the problems in too much or too intense presence? One of the difficulties is in oneself—one has to preserve one's own center from the fatigue and dispersal that come from too many demands. Some solitude is necessary for any human being to preserve his capacity for presence. Solitude deepens and clarifies it, while presence enriches and gives meaning to solitude. Paulus was jealous of his solitude. Like Nietzsche, he often got his best ideas while walking by the ocean or in the mountains, and it is not surprising that he prized these moments. His work schedule also assured him of solitude; that period from ten at night until two or three in the morning when he was all alone in his office was valued indeed.

But there is also a problem for others in withdrawing. One need not condone withdrawal from one's family, especially to the degree where it hurts them, in order to point out that there occasionally exists a man or woman who cannot bear the loss of freedom or the clipping of his or her wings that family life requires. Ralph Waldo Emerson wrote to the effect that he turned a deaf ear to friends, family members, and every other demand "when my genius calls me." Though this appears as ruthlessness, and often is, it is present in greater or lesser degree in every creative individual I have known.

I once stayed with the Tillich family for four or five days when I came to New York during my convalescence from tuberculosis. Paulus would sometimes pass me in the halls of their apartment, especially on arising in the morning, as though he had not seen me. I was surprised and resented the slight, and since that time have understood more deeply what Emerson meant. It was, of course, easier for an occasional visitor like myself to forgive than for Paulus' children who, for all their German heritage, did grow up in America.

Paulus was at the same time a man in whom loneliness was always present. It existed as an obbligato to his attendance at cocktail parties and social events which was almost compulsive at times. The feeling of aloneness was discernible even in his most intense moments of presence with someone he loved. Perhaps, as he was aware of the richness of human relationship, he was also more aware of the fact that it was so rare. To one woman he wrote, "You have come as near to the centre of my aloneness as it is perhaps humanly possible." This was meant, and was taken, as among the highest compliments Paulus could pay.

At times—though rarely—his intensity of presence reached a level which was difficult for his friends. One woman who loved him remarked to me that she was glad he had other women who could give to him also, because that took some of the weight off her. An experience of my own also illustrates how this presence can become too "heavy." One summer Hannah and Paulus were visiting us at our farm in New Hampshire. At first the weather was rainy, but when the gray sky turned to broken sunshine he and I decided to go sailing on Squam Lake. He enjoyed the "preliminaries," as he called them, of making the boat ready, hooking up the sail and putting on the rudder. He walked barelegged in the water around it with obvious pleasure.

We hoisted the sail and got under way with Paulus at the tiller while I bailed. When we were out on the lake, he told me how his father had taught him to sail on one of the lakes around Berlin ("When all the other boats turned over in a squall, we kept upright!").

But oddly, I found myself not up to the intensity of conversing with Paulus. I wanted to tone it down—it demanded too much of me. I felt trapped in the eighteen-foot sailboat; I needed some privacy, not to be thinking all the time. I achieved this by taking a brief nap in the boat, blocking off my consciousness for a spell.

This was the function of Hannah and my wife in the many conversations we four had. They absorbed some of the intensity.

Such intensity of consciousness *is* a real problem. One cannot have peak experience all the time, nor does anyone want to. Hence the infusion of Hindu meditation in our culture to give a constructive tone to solitude and to stop the machinery for a little while. Alcohol also serves to do this; it is a requirement, as Harry Stack Sullivan put it, of an industrial civilization, where it sets up a state of partial withdrawal from the mechanical pressure.

3

One important source of Paulus' personal presence was his high degree of centeredness in himself. He could accept into himself the negative aspects of the self, his finitude, the fact that he was going to die, his illnesses, his limitations of knowledge and energy. He absorbed these realities without flinching. It wasn't that he *liked* them—obviously he never did—but rather that he did not need to weaken himself by repressing these aspects of nonbeing. He was not fragmented by blocking off such parts of his personality. He is a good example of his own sentence in his *The Courage to Be*, "The self is the stronger the more non-being it can take into itself."

Once when he was seriously ill with trichinosis, I visited him in his darkened room in the Tillich apartment near the seminary. Paulus was lying flat in the middle of the bed, with his eyes closed, looking like a premature corpse. The room was as bare as a monk's cell, no books or magazines visible. I immediately expostulated sadly, "Oh, it's too bad you have to lie here in bed and can't even read."

"No, it's not bad at all," he answered with real relish in his voice but scarcely opening his eyes. "I can lie here hour after hour and just *be.*"

His personal presence was also markedly increased by his great knowledge. It will surprise some readers when I emphasize that a person confronts the world through his own symbols, and these are in fact based on all his knowledge at once, whether he is aware of it or not. Paulus encountered the world in many dimensions at the same time. He was at home with

Heraclitus in ancient Greece, with Abelard in the Middle Ages, and with Nicolas of Cusa in the Renaissance. He confronted a person with all these different levels at once. Many of the encounter groups in our time seek intimacy and intensity by cutting off the past and future, by truncating experience, by cutting the person *down* to intimacy. Paulus was an example of just the opposite: he came on not by checking his knowledge at the door but by inviting the person he met *up* to intimacy. In our day of "intimacy-over-the-weekend" we have forgotten the truth in Tennyson's "I am a part of all that I have met"—a fact which, since the advent of psychoanalysis, has become more cogent than even in Tennyson's day.

It is a kind of suicide—made possible only by our endemic despair in the Western world—to lop off all one knows and encounter others as though they and we had never had a past or would never have a future. Using one's knowledge to *avoid* the present is one thing: Paulus could rarely be accused of that. But using it to give depth to the present is an entirely other thing, and this was what made Paulus so direct and immediate: he came simultaneously with all his depth of the past thousands of years of Western tradition. He did not cut himself or yourself down to intimacy; he brought you up by challenging, by his perception and intuition, and by his sheer knowledge of the past and his hope for the future.

But his intense personal presence was also due to the fact that he could do no other. He needed human relationships to preserve his sanity. I have studied the Rorschach given Paulus by his friend, Frederic Spiegelberg of San Francisco. The startling thing about it is that his responses to the first cards, which are with one exception gray, led him into more and more acute anxiety. His world threatened to collapse. Only the later, colored cards brought him relief. These colors represent affective encounters; they come *at* one, so to speak, from the outside. He embraced them with great zest, for they gave him an affective structure, permitting him to form his world again. He had to have these relations of affect; they saved him personally from going down the road which would lead ultimately to psychological disintegration.

This bears especially on his relationships with women. They helped to give him a world of form and color. His great need of women led to his being particularly attractive to them. Out of this need also came the occasional compulsive element in his friendships and erotic relations. Noting this element, some persons have concluded that there was a dishonesty in Paulus, an insincerity in that he said what he did not wholly mean. This may have been true at rare times in his life, when his inner needs drove him to throw himself into the social whirl and make friends compulsively. But when a person wears his heart on his sleeve, he often appears superficially insincere but he is also unable to deceive others on any profound level. Hence the complications of Paulus' affective life led, paradoxically, to his extraordinary degree of psychological honesty.

Sigmund Freud wrote, "It may sound surprising that, due to my preoccupation with psychoanalysis, I cannot lie any more." Paulus once said to his students that because he did not know English well, "I cannot play any tricks of language upon you." And because of the psychological problems noted above and his preoccupation with them, he could not play tricks upon us in the larger, human sense.

CHAPTER 4

The Death
of His Mother

Paulus was born in 1876, the oldest of three children. His sister
Johanna was three years younger, and his other sister, Elis-
abeth, seven years younger. His father, who left his Lutheran
pastorate to take a position of leadership in the German
Church, was from Brandenburg in eastern Germany and his
mother from the Rhineland. The father, according to Hannah,
was a "gruff, charming, instructive, ambitious man." I shall post-
pone my main discussion of Paulus' relation with him until a
later chapter.

But the mother! The more I consider her, the more convincingly I understand the origin of the fact that Paulus' relationships with women were colorful, rich, problematical, secretive,
and difficult to comprehend. Other people found his mother
enigmatic: most persons who knew her hesitated to talk about
her. In the photographs I have seen she appears reserved, shy,
and beautiful in a quiet way. But most important of all she
exudes a strength like the Pacific Ocean: calm and quiet on the
surface but tremendously powerful underneath. While the father fussed, fumed, and assumed the tones of the strong one, it
is very clear that he did not have the final say; the mother was
the power behind the throne.

Not only did Paulus worship her, but he possessed her so far
as a child can. The first and only male child, at the age of one
year he sits on his mother's arm in the old photographs like a
cock of the walk, confident and assured of his place in the
universe. He is as supreme here as he seemed later as a young
man, sitting on the thrones of sand he was wont to make for
himself on the shore of the North Sea. In these early photos, he
asserts himself and his primacy, we have no difficulty in imagin-
ing his later greatness. His sister Johanna later was to join in the
adoration of her good-looking brother.

As one would expect, his relation to his mother had a strong
influence on Paulus' sexual development. He planned as a small
boy to marry this woman he adored, and while it is common for
children to want to marry their parent of the opposite sex,
Paulus maintained the assumption deeper and longer than
most. When he was small, one may assume he had much sexual
energy, as he did at every later stage of his life. But how could
this Victorian mother accept sex in her infant even on an entirely unconscious level—especially since in the playful fantasy
of both he was *her* lover? Paulus must have picked up with his
mother's milk the feeling she wished him to have: that sexual
impulses are bad and unacceptable in public and must be kept
a secret. This is not to be confused with the repression that
occurs typically in the American child where the blocking takes
place on the level of feeling. Paulus was later to wonder how
we in America managed to preserve any spontaneity and vitality at all in the face of our radical repression of bodily feelings.
But in Germany there is often present a lustiness and heartiness
of emotion, as shown for example in Luther's enthusiastic
familiarity with fornication and defecation. For Paulus, at any
rate, what was required was a suppression of the act but not the
fantasy. Sex was clearly admitted but furtive: its impulses could
be felt but should not be acted upon.

His energy as a small boy was thus shifted from sex to knowledge. This is not a difficult jump, since the two are already so richly related in myth and literature. He was always greatly intrigued by the Garden of Eden myth and often spoke of the identification of sex and knowledge in the story of Adam and Eve. Here the attainment of sexual knowledge is used as a kind of synonym for the gaining of all knowledge. In Tillich's discussions in class I first learned that the ancient words for sexual intercourse in both Hebrew and Greek were the same as the word for knowledge. "Abraham *knew* his wife, and she conceived," is the construction we encounter time and again. The myth of Faust is another example of the connection: Faust (who in some ways resembles Paulus) was promised both sexual conquest and knowledge by Mephistopheles.

For a child with Paulus' sensitivity and intelligence, the substitution of knowledge for sex was a "natural." This meant that eros—in which knowledge and sex both participate and which is already partly an idealization of sex—was precociously developed in his personality. I have heard of no sexual games while he was a child, no "playing doctor" with neighboring children. Indeed, his specifically sexual development seems to have been delayed; I find him in his teens naïve about sexuality as such. The absorption of his early sexual ardor into a passion for knowledge seems in fact to have worked all too well. Hence he was to feel in later life that, erotically speaking, he had to make up for lost time.

2

All through his life Paulus was to approach women with a confidence which testified to his feeling successful acceptance in the arms of his mother, and an assurance—which was amply demonstrated—that other women would love him as well. Here we can see the beginning of trends that are to follow Paulus throughout his life: secretiveness about sex and the inability to devote himself single-mindedly to the one woman to whom he was married.

It is all in all a common picture: the great man emerges from an infancy and childhood in which he is not only fortunate in natural endowments but also favored by some tacit, close understanding with his mother. Sigmund Freud is another example of it. Like knowledge of his aristocratic lineage in a prince, the awareness that a deep rapport exists with one's own mother can be a source of profound psychological and spiritual strength.

This intimate relation with his mother seems to throw light on Paulus' great interest in the motherly function in all other women. When Hannah was pregnant he was very involved, and when she gave birth to their daughter Erdmuthe Paulus was beside himself with curiosity and concern. He looked at the baby's tiny hands in amazement. He loved Mutie, as she was called, especially when she was very small—he used to delight in taking her out in the carriage and showing her off. When David and Ellie Roberts were staying at East Hampton, Paulus often baby-sat with their newly born child, remarking to Ellie how "astonishable" (as he used to misstate the word) it was to feel this other being in the same room with him.

When Paulus was seventeen, his mother died of a painful form of cancer, melanoma. This was for him surely the most important formative event up to that time, and in some ways of all his life. At her death he felt the whole world disappear from under his feet. In all its concrete vividness he experienced the reality of nothingness. Where was the mother who furnished the rudder a strong love gives? He had depended upon her, and she was no longer there. Where there ought to have been someone, indeed the most important one, now there was no one. Shattered were the great confidence and the unconscious faith that behind all the vicissitudes of life there remained Mother. Not only did he experience a great bereavement, but he felt profoundly abandoned and betrayed. His orientation to the universe was gone; there was no longer any up or down.

At that time Paulus wrote the following poem:

> Am I then I? who tells me that I am!
> Who tells me what I am, what I shall become?
> What is the world's and what life's meaning?
> What is being and passing away on earth?
>
> O abyss without ground, dark depth of madness!
> Would that I had never gazed upon you and were
> sleeping like a child![1]

The poem is a veritable "to be or not to be,"[2] with no one to answer the question now that his mother was gone. It speaks out of the depth of loneliness, grief, and his missing of her. Yet it does not deal specifically with the loss of a mother but with the loss of himself; it is the eruption of an extreme crisis in identity. His mother could have told him who and what he is. But she is now dead.

It is a pathetic picture: the young man barely out of boyhood standing on the edge of the abyss and crying out questions with no one there to answer. Asking the question of what he is means also asking what he is to become; it is a necessary corollary. He desperately yearns to know his own significance, his value to the

---

1. The German original follows:

> Bin ich denn ich, wer sagt mir, dass ich bin!
> Wer sagt mir, was ich bin, was ich soll werden
> Was ist der Welten, was des Lebens Sinn?
> Was ist das Sein und das Vergehn auf Erden?
>
> O Abgrund ohne Grund, des Wahnsinns finstre Tiefe!
> Ach dass ich nimmer Dich geschaut
> und kindlich schliefe!

2. The suggestion of Hamlet is unmistakable. By this time Paulus had read the play, which became his favorite drama. Not much later, at twenty, he memorized the whole of it word for word.

world, and his value to her, which is now—sadly—relevant only in memory because she is dead. All his goals and aims and shining hopes, where are they now? The meaning of the world and life, indeed the meaning of death: they all are among the questions he hurls out.

He does not call on God—though the questions are of that ultimate character. He calls on the one who was most starkly real and concrete, the mother who bore and nourished him, who gave him being to begin with, but who now can no longer speak to him. As Nietzsche exclaimed only a few decades earlier when he also felt there was no longer any north or south: ". . . this earth [is unchained] from its sun." We fall backward, "sideways, forward, in all directions . . . we feel the breath of empty space . . . night and more night is coming on all the while."[3] It is no accident that in describing Tillich's youthful experience of the death of his mother, I think of Nietzsche's lament on the death of God.

The poem, then, shows his realization that he stands on the verge of the "dark depth of madness." Gazing too long into the abyss—an infinite abyss "without ground"—leads to the borders of insanity. It is a point we shall return to later: Can a man ask the question of existence too strongly or too persistently, so that in fact he finds himself on the edge of madness? How much consciousness can a human being bear?

You can look into the abyss, but you cannot throw yourself into it—you need, indeed, some escort, some Virgil such as Dante had in his trip into the circles of hell. A therapist needs some other therapist to take along when he goes psychologically into the depths of schizophrenia—to preserve his sanity, to guarantee his horizon, a beacon to keep clear his north and south. But Paulus had lost his beacon.

The last line is completely human, though strange in that

3. Walter Kaufman, *Nietzsche* (New York: Princeton University Press, 1956).

context. *If I had never looked into the abyss,* he cries. If I never expected more, if I had remained in the Garden of Eden and had never been born to consciousness, anxiety, and responsibility—*I would be sleeping as a child.* It is the radical regression that from time to time tempts us all, though rarely stated as vividly as here. He would go back to the age when he *did* have his mother; the age before the fall, the age when he was secure and untroubled by all the soul-tormenting questions. This means giving up his eros for knowledge, giving up the splendid plans that must have sprung partly from his desire to be worthy of his mother's love. For that is gone now; he wishes he could close his eyes, shut off the most spiritual organ, and sleep like a child.

There is a certain prediction in this poem. For Paulus *did* keep the childlike side of himself, did remain boyish all through life. My picture of him as a child-lion in that first meeting with him is appropriate. His attractiveness to women all his life is also related to it. One sleeps like a child; this is appealing to everyone. Paulus always carried along the child in him, the aspect of himself that came from the time when he did have a mother.

I assume that the questions about his own being and the questions of his mother go hand in hand. He can now never find the answer to the query: What does my mother in her secret heart think of me and my father? Does she love me more than she loves Father? What is the secret place she keeps for me? What goes on in her heart about my father?

Could he never now supplant his father in her eyes, since she was already dead? Only in his little-boy self was it possible to keep her, to win her. And that he had done, and was to do later with other women.

The death of his mother shook his mental life to its very roots, forcing him to give up his preoccupation with fantasy and accept the reality of the world. It was at this time that he formed his ideal of becoming a philosopher.

3

The shock of his mother's death struck Paulus when his inner life was already set in conflict. He bore in his blood the contrast between eastern and western Germany, which he saw as a tension between his father and mother. There is still alive, he writes of his father's origin, "in eastern Germany an inclination toward meditation tinged with melancholy, a heightened consciousness of duty and personal sin, a strong regard for authority and feudal traditions. . . . Western Germany [from which his mother came] is characterized by a zest for life, love of the concrete, mobility, rationality and democracy."[4]

This tension certainly existed in Paulus. But we have already found that the problem is more complex. In his mother we saw not a carefree, fun-loving person but one noble in mien and enigmatic. The spontaneity may have been there, but the power was also. Thus for even more cogent reasons than he cites, Paulus could truly say with Faust, "Two souls, alas, within me dwell."

In this inner tension we can see the beginning of his perpetual affinity for living on the boundary between opposing forces, at the hazardous time of their encounter. All his life he seems to have liked to stir up a "witch's brew," as Hannah put it when she was critical. Such a brew was his identification with persons in complex difficulties with each other, who used to come to him for guidance, or his fascination with philosophical problems which looked well-nigh insoluble to the rest of us. He could thus discover the hidden elements in the "brew," which, by his stirring, were forced to the surface. He was right in believing that when human beings are in conflict, the unconscious tendencies which are normally kept like horses in their stalls come out to cavort.

4. Paul Tillich, *On the Boundary* (New York: Charles Scribner's Sons, 1966), p. 14.

He lived perpetually in *Angst*. But most of it he would have regarded as normal anxiety coming from an inescapable fate, and partly also the anxiety of the creative person. Living in tension was a concomitant of life for him and his kind. There was a "constant and tense contest between these paternal and maternal influences," he writes in one autobiographical sketch. "Again and again an eruption would be necessary to give these elements room, and often the eruptions would lead to extremes." He describes himself as living "in the midst of struggle and fate," of "two principles wrestling with each other." Hence in his philosophy of history he preferred to see truth as dynamic, the result of pitting two opposing principles against each other. "Truth is found in the midst of struggle and destiny, not, as Plato taught, in an unchanging beyond."[5]

No one could ever speak of Paulus as "adjusted." Or if one did one would have to say he was most adjusted when his maladjustments were closest to the surface. The term "adjusted personality" would have had no positive meaning for him, and if you had used it in his presence he would have grimaced. "Classical composure and harmony were not part of my heritage," he confesses. That is why the classical aspect of Goethe was alien to him, and why he always appreciated the preclassical culture of ancient Greece—the philosophies of Heraclitus and Empedocles more than Plato's, and the sculpture of the archaic period more than that of Phidias or Praxiteles.

That is also why, despite his Germanic vocabulary, he always seemed to me to be the most contemporary of my teachers. Like the rest of us in the twentieth century, he had to live Dionysian and think Apollonian, and he seemed to have been born to do precisely that. These built in conflicts kept him always psychologically open and dynamic. His existence seemed like a man riding a bicycle who keeps his equilibrium by constant forward movement.

5. Ibid., p. 15.

But it would be unfair not to mention the fact that, though composure and complacency were foreign to Tillich, there did emanate from his face and personality a sense of peace. It was a dynamic peace, like the surface of his ocean at East Hampton when the colors change in the evening. In Paulus it was a peace which comes from seeing meaning in the most chaotic states, a peace which comes from the courage to meet the "devils" head on. Modern art such as that of Pollock and Motherwell appealed to him. They literally paint tension, and their paintings are never quiet but have a peace which comes only from dynamic equilibrium. Paulus considered the sentimental academic art of the late nineteenth century, especially in most churches, dishonest, not deserving the title of art at all. With courage he could meet the most profound despair—including his own death—and still believe and hope. Whenever I was in despair myself I longed to be near Paulus, for I knew that no matter how deep my discouragement, he had gone deeper.

4

"No idea is true," exclaims Nietzsche, "unless it is thought in the open air." Tillich's thirst for nature and love of the out-of-doors was born among the hills of eastern Germany. All his life, his sense of wonder would be ignited, and his sensitive imagination set off by almost any natural scene. Once when he and Hannah visited us in New Hampshire, we took them on a hike up Rattlesnake Mountain and sat at the top looking out over island-spotted, blue-green Squam Lake. Long after the rest of us had had our fill of the view, Paulus implored us to stay a little longer so that, lying on the rocks, he could continue to gaze out at the mountains and the water.

In East Hampton there was abundant natural beauty surrounding his house. In one of his letters he wrote: "Apple trees and lilacs are blooming at the same time. The ocean is very beautiful, and the lawn is an intensively green carpet. It is good to be here. . . ." He gloried in the rain: "The greatest blessing for me (and for the lawn) is the large amount of rain we have had this year. The growth of the trees in our 'park' is incredible. Everything is as beautiful as it ever was before. The grace of rain. . . ." (What poetry in that last sentence!)

How he loved to watch the ocean at night, especially during or after a storm (preferably a hurricane) when the sea pounded with full fury against the shore! When my wife and I went out to East Hampton to see the Tillichs, arriving on a Friday night, Paulus could not wait to hurry us down to the lighthouse, to stand on the breakwater just out of reach of the gigantic black waves smashing against the rocks in white foam. There was a seductive and bewitching rhythm, a magnificent daimonic power crashing in white and black against the surrounding seawall. This would send Paulus into ecstasy: a fiendish force commensurate with his own deepest power which also struggled at the point of encounter between chaos and cosmos.

Yet Paulus was no sentimentalist about nature. He knew full well, and said so repeatedly, that nature has nothing to offer us except what we bring to it. I take this to mean that the structure, the forms, the archetypes in the human being are also in nature. We can, with our capacity for self-consciousness, project ourselves on nature. The more we sense its beauty, the more we can identify with it. Since we too participate in the basic structure of nature, we thus see ourselves at a deeper level. We feel various emotions: comfort, relief from our loneliness, and a fellow feeling, a feeling of being understood—which means understanding ourselves at a deeper level. Nature is a variegated screen calling forth our own projections. But to call it a "screen" does not mean that it is dead; it means that we must ourselves bring the capacity to "see in nature what is ours," as Wordsworth aptly put it.

Paulus, indeed, had much to bring. He had the capacity, for

which Socrates is the prototype, of giving himself over in a kind
of trance to nature about him. Whatever the view—whether
the chaotic lights of New York City from the high window of my
office or the waves of the ocean in East Hampton—he experienced the external world as a boon, a backdrop against
which he could feel his deepest sorrow and joy. This brought his
frequently tormented spirit some comfort and relief from grief.

CHAPTER 5

Eros

The most difficult if fascinating side of Tillich's life to write
about is his love for women and their love for him. I feel that
whatever I write will be misunderstood—as it must be. But a
more serious doubt which gnaws at me is that whatever I write
will be inadequate to the task of conveying the quality of this
love. Risking what must be risked, however, I shall nevertheless
try to portray this critical aspect of his life as best I can.

The simple fact is that he was a remarkably lovable man. He
had a spiritual quality combined with sensuousness which
women found highly attractive. Wilhelm Pauck tells us that in
Germany in his younger days women would swarm about him
after every lecture. The same was true in New York and at
Harvard; wherever he spoke, women gathered around. He ex-
ercised upon them the daimonic fascination which Goethe says
is given for no fathomable reason to certain men and not to
others. I speak specifically of women; I never encountered or
heard of any homosexual activity on Paulus' part. What I am
referring to was experienced particularly by women and felt by
Paulus to refer to them.

A young woman who came under Paulus' erotic spell wrote
a poem to him after hearing him give a lecture:

My eyes go from the clouds to you to the stars,
And thus I weave a cradle for you.

The two lines say what many women before her and multitudes after sensed without being aware of it: the childlike quality in him. In one way he was a little boy whom women yearned to take care of. But from another side he was the man of great mind who took them on journeys through vast solar systems of ideas. Attracted by the childlike element, they were then rewarded with Paulus' powerful emotions and penetrating insights. "I weave a cradle for you" is aptly put; it reminds us of the last line in his own poem, "Would I were sleeping like a child."

Paulus could also draw women into his life by his extraordinary capacity for fantasy. When I was a senior at the seminary he gave a lecture one spring afternoon at a college near the city where the young woman lived to whom I was engaged. I had introduced them briefly when she was in New York. She attended the lecture and spoke to Paulus afterward. It being a sunny afternoon, he invited her to go for a walk with him over the campus. They sat down under a tree and he then began a fantasy, inviting her to join him. As was his custom, he wove into it elves, trolls, and all sorts of imagined wood sprites, somewhat on the order of Tolkien. The two of them seemed to be living in a primitive land of wood folk, and the theme obviously caught my fiancée's imagination as well as his. At one point Paulus asked, "And what would we do then?" She—who was not one to suggest such things lightly—answered, "We would lie together."

The day after seeing her Tillich stopped me in the corridor and said, "I want to thank you for the marvelous hour I spent with Miss Bronson." My own feelings were the same as when she phoned me about it: I was glad both of them had had their delightful hour. I was a little proud of the event, and had no jealousy. Though nothing physical occurred, it was a kind of psychological reenactment of the old custom of the deflowering of the new bride by the Lord of the Estate. I *was* a little jealous, however, of Paulus' capacity for such imaginative fantasies.

This incident shows the extraordinary web of emotional power he could weave over a woman. It was a sensual seduction, not a sexual one; the distinction is crucial. Another man might easily have turned the spiritual seduction into a physical one. Not Paulus—and not simply out of prudence or because it is considered bad form to seduce the fiancée of one of your students. He was genuinely devoted to the sensual in life by contrast with the sexual. He left the woman very much attached to him; consequently there were over the country a growing number of them who carried a torch for Tillich. Most of them kept it faithfully lit, like Solveig in *Peer Gynt,* and prized it in their secret hearts. A few resented the "unfinished business" and would have preferred carrying love through to some culmination.

Among them all there was a remarkable lack of jealousy of each other. When Paulus was in the hospital with the illness from which he died, women of whom I had never heard telephoned me from various parts of the country to inquire about him, and I always marveled at their lack of jealousy. It was not that they did not know there were others. But each spoke out of her own conviction that she represented something special to Paulus—some unique insight, revelation, or secret kind of relationship which occurred in some particular hour or walk together.

The strange thing is that each was probably right. There was generally a special contribution from and to Paulus which did not get confused with his relationships with others. "He had enough eros for all," as one woman put it. So far did the interest of women in Paulus extend! This indicates again that the center of the attraction was not sex, which can be and generally is a quantitative thing; when it is given to one, we do not have it to give to another. *Eros* and the love which is esteem, agape, on the other hand, expand as they grow and normally nourish everyone they touch.

There were many dimensions to his loving. One was the sheer sexual libido which emanated from him; this cannot go unmentioned even though it did not figure predominantly in his aims. The wife of a friend of mine worked as a secretary at Harvard while Tillich was teaching there. She remarked with some amazement to her husband that when he came down the hall, though he was then seventy years old, he was always the "sexiest" man in the whole place.

We must keep in mind that Paulus and Hannah were emigrés from the Weimar Republic, which against a background of despair had produced a strange contradiction of exuberance on the one hand—always in the shadow of death—and decadence on the other. The culture in which they moved there was self-consciously Freudian; they were well aware of the rediscovery of the body, and they hungered to be part of this revolution before it was too late. Also Paulus' first marriage must be seen in this picture: he had been married, in his naïveté, to the mother of a friend, a woman considerably older than himself, before he went off to World War I. While he was away at war another friend (who had first introduced the young Paulus to heterosexual sex) seduced his wife. She was carrying the other man's child when he returned from the war. It is surely a background calculated to produce a very high degree of sexual frustration.

The sexual urge, however, was in the service of another aim which I call, in its strict sense, eros. Paulus' life was the clearest demonstration of eros in action I have ever seen. His relationships were always a pull toward a higher state, an allure of new forms, new potentialities, new nuances of meaning, in promise if not in actuality. In one of his letters to an intimate friend he writes, "My mind is always wandering between life and death, hope and despair about the ultimate. I understand now why in the last scene of Faust II, Faust is saved by Gretchen from above. This is the way I look at you." This reference to Faust illustrates an extreme form of eros.

In another letter he takes a further and unmistakable step in giving a divine function to woman.

If you can affirm your life, you can accept your death, and conversely. But I doubt whether I can do either. Sometimes when I feel this very deeply I say to myself, "But she (meaning you) loves me" and it is as if you stand as the accepting priest, representing the divine voice . . . not by saying anything but by being what you are and loving me.

Thus the beloved woman is the way to God, playing a role not unlike Mary in Roman Catholicism. Paulus had said earlier, "Women are closer to God." This foreshadows some of the problems that will come up later in our discussion of his eroticism.

One of the qualities with which he endows eros, and the loved woman, is the capacity to constitute him as a being. Paulus' own emotional and ontological needs were great, and he demanded from women—in a direct line from his relationship to his mother—that they meet these needs. I say ontological because he required constant support and reassurance for his being. In one of his letters to a woman whom he loved authentically and deeply he writes, in a note just before Easter, "All my vitality resurrects if I think of you. Think of me on Easter morning! Will the stone ever be rolled away? Infinite love, P."

Another time he thanks her for "pushing the demons away" and continues, "I draw into me your warmth, your being! I have continuous changes of jubilant and depressive moods. In both of them I would like to have you as near as possible to me!"

He had a way of looking not *at* but *into* a woman, with his attention fully concentrated on her. This fascinated women. It was not a seducer's approach—or, if you wish to use the word, it was a spiritual seduction. The intensity of presence gave a security to the woman as well as the experience of being fully known, united with him. He also had remarkable intuition, a capacity to see into the being of the other person, to know her psychological and emotional yearnings, hopes, and fears, and to see in a woman potentialities which she did not yet know existed. His way of speaking in conversation or in lectures, especially when he discussed love in its various forms, gripped one with the revelation of something new in one's own emotions; it seemed so profound and so true that women received an assurance which led them to advance toward him with a courage which surprised even themselves.

Most women were disarmed, taken off their usual guard, by his intense presence. Made slightly giddy by the anxiety that comes with the discovery of new possibilities, they felt a pleasant embarrassment and the dizziness of mild anxiety. With Paulus they would open their emotions and feel they were led into new worlds, where there were new visions and new sensations. They felt the encounter as one of the most treasured experiences of their lives, and kept it in memory as a mixture of dream and reality which had its own separate existence. Objectively, he did give them a kind of individuality which resulted in their carrying themselves with greater self-confidence. Subjectively, in Paulus' presence, they knew something they never had known before, and they clung to his conversation and the look in his eyes as one does to a love letter.

A strict Freudian would have called Paulus' intimacy with women sublimation, a term he himself never liked; he regarded it as the most puritanical concept in all of Freud. I think it will be clear that his sensuality does not fit the term but is something distinct.

One woman who had been a dear friend of Paulus for some

years stopped to see him in East Hampton. Having only two hours between trains, she walked with him by the sea—the richest way, he always felt, to spend a short time. She was impressed by the fact that he kept a tight grip on her hand every moment of the time. The bodily contact seemed terribly important to him. His letters to his women friends were filled with such words as "touch," "light," "warmth," "glow," and other terms which express sensuality rather than sexuality. Passion he had, to be sure; but he sought the warm glow of it, aided by a powerful imagination, rather than its physical actuality.

Secrecy was another essential trait of Paulus' erotic life. His sexual feelings had begun in relation to a strong mother, and they must be kept veiled. Secrecy surrounded the whole area: secrecy from his father, from the public, from all the world except Mother. The women who succeeded with Paulus were those who had and kept secrets with him. The veiled quality was necessary for the relationship to survive.

He could talk about sexuality in public so long as it was not personal confession. And talk about it he did, with a frankness and honesty which stood out radically indeed in faculties where most professors spoke as if they had never heard the word sex. It was in Paulus' lectures that I first heard of the "love bite," that moment of hostility and aggression which occurs at the climax in sexual intercourse. He believed that, even though partly aggressive, the sexual act in the orgasm is still a giving of the persons to each other. It is the tension between the aggressiveness and the giving which produces the ecstasy of sex. From Paulus I also heard of the "union of opposites," of which sexual intercourse is a symbol—the straining of the totality of one person to become wholly absorbed in the other person. But in his lectures there was nothing of his personal erotic life.

Secrecy, I have said, but not dishonesty. Honesty is the accurate recognition within oneself of feelings and the consequences of one's behavior. This Paulus certainly had. I have never heard of his telling an actual untruth in this regard; he was singularly free of repression or self-deceit. When some person was hurt by Paulus—which outside his family was rare indeed—it was generally from the fact that he could not, in human time and space, see one and not another, walk with one without slighting another. This was another reason why the secrecy was essential.

Most of his reaching out to women was done by his eyes and voice. He gazed at each one as though looking for someone. He drank each one in. What was he hunting for? Each could be the fountain for his thirst.

2

It must now be obvious that Paulus was seeking his lost mother. I do not mean this to explain the quality of his loving, which owes much more to the genuine trust his mother originally gave him. But the hypothesis of his seeking the vanished mother does cast light on the slightly compulsive quality of the search and the insatiability of his loving. This quest is carried on against a backdrop of relationship with her which was close, strong, and absorbing, in the security of which his self could grow and expand. This mother who loved him later abandoned him. After her death when he was seventeen, we would expect him to look at women and wonder whether and in what ways they were like his mother. Then, through experiencing the success of such a way with women, he could grow into his larger pattern with them, which greatly enriched both himself and the women he met and loved.

As I write this, I think, How like Adam and Eve in the garden! Originally a situation of "innocence"; and later the fall, the loneliness, being thrown on one's own into all the problems to which human flesh is heir. Paulus' existentialism was by no

means simply a set of ideas, and though it may have emerged
in that horrendous night on the battlefield, it was not born
there. It was born when his mother died. The whole concept of
an original good *essence* followed by the fall into *existence* is
here in its rough outline. It is basic not only for his existentialism
but for his theology and his treatment of the myth of Adam and
Eve as well. The questions of existence, which can be asked
because of a previous essence, then lead us in Paulus' writing
back to the essence of the "new being." Creation, fall, and
salvation are summarized in Paulus' own life.

Except, of course, that life is infinitely more complex than
theory. What we are concerned with at the moment is the
vicissitudes of the phase called existence, the endless—or almost endless—quest to be saved by Gretchen, as Goethe puts
it, or by "the mothers" as he puts it elsewhere in Faust.

Paulus often found one particular woman to ally himself with,
in actuality but even more in imagination, when working on a
book or preparing a lecture. This was done quite consciously: he
remarked once that he could not write a book without having
a woman in mind to write it for. He would write it, however,
out of himself and his insights; he would not be influenced by
her. Then he would say, "This book is for *you.*"

This is the living out of an age-old myth, an archetype which
goes back many aeons: that one brings his trophies back to the
adored woman as Lancelot sought to bring the Holy Grail back
to Queen Guinevere. It does not disparage our deeds or emotions, certainly not those of Paulus, to see them in this vast
perspective; it dignifies them. Hannah once showed us, as
Paulus sat by enthusiastically approving, some watercolor sketches she had done in which she was making love in a meadow
while all her ancestors grew out of the trees of the surrounding
forest like a Greek chorus to celebrate the event. A long cho-
reography of human achievements links us to past generations;
we are bound to our own childhood in the same way as our

children will be bound to us. The concept makes a bond between human beings; we are no longer so lonely or so isolated.
I am confident Paulus would have agreed with this. It is one of
the things that makes the stage of human existence endurable.

Paulus seems to have been psychologically incapable of in-
vesting his love openly and completely in the one woman
whom he married. We can understand this partially also from
his original relation with his mother: his passion must be kept
secret. A marriage is too public. Also, his mother was powerful
and Paulus had considerable dependence on her. This absorbed
too much of his autonomy, caged him too much. This is not
infrequently true of men who have developed extraordinary
ability in several areas, far ahead of their growth in other
realms. To the extent that they mature successfully, they must
disinfect this close relationship typically with the mother, fight
it off, achieve their autonomy by their own declaration of independence. Paulus' mother died, and he could never do this
successfully. So he was continuously ambivalent about the stage
of marriage and had to protest against its bonds. On the very
night of their marriage, he demonstrated his independence by
going off with his bachelor friends.

One woman once remarked to me, "No woman would have
made a good wife to Paulus." His emotions were too complex,
his needs too great, and his withdrawal too habitual. Hannah
succeeded in many ways and failed in some. But the fantasy of
innumerable women, "If I had been married to Paulus, things
would have been different!" seems to me largely a delusion.
Hannah's sharp insight and her very active intelligence were
necessary to him; even her hostile criticism, at times seemed
also in a strange way something he needed. Although she partially met the problem by having friends of her own outside the
marriage, she still naturally suffered much from Paulus' devotion to other women. He recognized this and, so far as one can,
consciously bore the guilt. Perhaps he had his relationship with

Hannah in mind when he said that a person's conscience cannot
be both sensitive and good at the same time.

One strategy open to a person who is married but smarts
under it is to withdraw psychologically. This Paulus did. His
withdrawal was also part of the process of his thinking and
intuition, i.e., his creativity. I do not know any authentically
creative person who does not insist on his times of solitude.

Once I visited Hannah and Paulus in East Hampton after
going through the sad and bitter experience of a divorce. During that weekend he and I walked along the shore of the ocean,
as was his custom. Just before our meeting, he had received a
letter from a woman who was a dear friend of both of us, and
afterward wrote her mentioning my having been there and
having spoken with enthusiasm of seeing her. Then he went on:

My advice to you is not to press for marriage, even in the most subtle
way. The truth is Rollo does not want it now with anyone.
    He wants to watch the waves of the ocean and of life. I looked at him
—and I saw myself!

                                                    Love,
                                                        P.

It is true that I was going through the process of re-forming
oneself which occurs after a divorce, and that this required a
time of withdrawal; it was temporary and later largely over-
come. But the important phrase in the letter is about Paulus:
"I saw myself." He is aware of his vocation of watching the
waves of the ocean and of the human scene, and knows that it
requires standing aside from the cares and pressures of life.
Hence the Roman Catholic Church, with a wisdom not often
appreciated in these days of group mindedness and other
means of huddling together in our anxiety, has required celi-
bacy for those of its clergy who, like Thomas Merton, need it.

It is of course easier for me, and for others who profited
greatly and drank deeply from Paulus' mind and spirit, to for-

give this than for his wife and son and daughter, who faced his detachment more continuously. His children had to bear the brunt of knowing that he had sensitivity and eros in abundance for hundreds of other persons in the world but not much for them. When he traveled he remarked in letters how encumbered he felt with the family, and how much freer he felt—in Paris, for example—when he was alone. He was subject to a compulsive need to protect his own creative solitude; he smarted under the loss of space to maneuver which a family entails.

Not until late in life was he able to invest enough of his trust and love in Hannah to make a satisfying and mutually supportive relationship. Then he did. Thus he dedicates the last volume of his *Systematic Theology* "To Hannah, Companion of my Life."

3

The potentially destructive effect of his erotic life was to cause Paulus a great deal of concern. A truly daimonic element was involved in his attitudes and behavior toward women. When speaking of a portrait painter for whom he had been sitting, he called this element in the painting "my ambiguity," "my dark spiritual shadows." The death of his mother had left him psychologically and spiritually destitute, with no meaningful world in which to orient himself. Women who could lead him back into the world were extraordinarily valued in Paulus' myth of life. They were made into creatures who possessed the power of salvation. We saw his Easter letter (p. 53). He wrote to the same woman: "You are a human being as fragile as myself. But I almost pray, Have mercy! . . . While I am writing this a wave of love rises in me, and even if this letter could never reach you, it would be a release from overwhelming sorrow."

But we know that when people worship other human beings

there must be a balancing negation. If a person is made into a
God, he is also made into a devil; the evil side is pushed forward,
as always happens with the daimonic. If a person worships
women, he cannot help sometimes also destroying them. The
feelings of need for revenge are present in Paulus.

In this way, too, the close relationship with his mother took
its toll. Paulus had a recurrent dream, "My mother kept me
dancing on a coin." When as an adult he told his father this
dream, the latter burst into tears. This suggests that the father
knew all too well the mother's stubbornness and authority.
When early in their marriage Paulus and Hannah had living
with them a friend who was in analytic training, Paulus under-
took a short psychoanalysis. One day he came running out of the
room toward Hannah to strangle her. Such pronounced hostility must come from somewhere, and bespeaks a need to kill off
the woman to protect one's own autonomy. Psychologically
speaking, this was partly to gain his freedom from the too close
tie to his mother—a fight against the situation which resulted
in her taking his whole world with her when she died.

Partly it is also an expression of his rage at being abandoned;
there was no place to "sleep like a child." While he greatly
appreciated the "madonna" side of women, he also from time
to time saw them as prostitutes. He could give them individuality but he also could heap them into a nameless mass. He could
distinguish them and also extinguish them. He could put them
into the "bottomless abyss" he wrote of in his poem—he could
make them taste the "dark depth of madness."

At this point the reader may have hesitation in going along
with my story. I can only agree that it is exceedingly difficult,
often impossible, to admit that we all possess these daimonic
tendencies, or that Oscar Wilde's line, "Each man kills the thing
he loves," was written about you and me. In dealing with people like Paulus, we tend to slide back into the assumption that
with the removal of a few minor aberrations, the worshiped

person would fit our ideal and could then be worshiped without contradiction. Thus we exploit him or her, the very one we worship! We overlook the evil in ourselves and others so that we can the better worship the ideal figure—which is our way of repressing awareness of our own imperfections. We do not, then, permit the "great" man to have his human freedom and frailties. Our need to worship overcomes our respect for truth. If there is one thing against which Paulus had sworn eternal enmity, it was precisely this!

I will here try to follow the course Paulus would have wished: to speak the truth without garnishing it, but also maintain a sense of proportion about his life.

In the society in which Paulus grew up, the custom in school was to punish a person by adding humilitation to pain. The teacher would take down a boy's pants and expose his buttocks to the class as he paddled him. The maids would ask Paulus when he got home from school, "Were you beaten today?" with prurient expressions on their faces, and then ask lasciviously, "Did you enjoy it?" It was this kind of sexual mores that led German intellectual society after World War I, to which Hannah and Paulus belonged, to rebel against all bourgeois sexual morality. The intellectuals not only took the Freudian revolution seriously; they also saw the implications. They were aware that in the best of us all evils are potentially present, while in the worst of us—in criminals, for example—the most saintly deeds are also present as potentialities. It was a time when Luther's advice to Melanchthon was surely relevant, "Sin bravely but believe more bravely."

With women he could not reach in other ways, there came out in Paulus' behavior a sadistic tendency. This expressed itself in seeking a higher, rarefied kind of pleasure in pain.[1] He un-

---

1. Some of this sadism can be interpreted psychoanalytically. If the mother dies, the child is bound to ask the question, "Did she not love me?" (If she had, she would not have left me.) It is not too far a jump to the feeling "If I had killed

derstood Nietzsche's statement, "When thou goest to women,
take thy whip." It was a physical pain which has all the sensuous
refinement of a Marquis de Sade. Pleasure and pain are in fact
much closer together than our culture admits: the idea that
they are opposites has seemed to me at times superficial and at
other times downright silly. Socrates told us long ago that pleasure is increased by pain; for example, being hungry, which is
a pain, adds to the pleasure of eating. Paulus knew that it was
not by accident that at the climax of sexual intercourse there
are *both* pleasure and a heightened experience of pain, exqui-
sitely merged.

Paulus never to my knowledge visited a prostitute for the
purpose of explicit sexual experience. But he often went to talk
with them, showing by his action that he had no condemnation
of them. When my former wife and I went with the Tillichs to
see the play *The Iceman Cometh*, he was enthralled by the
similarity between my wife and one of the prostitutes in the
drama. She seems to have liked the idea, and experienced it not
as a degrading comparison but as one bringing out the great
variety of forms of sexuality.

Paulus greatly disliked dirty or sexual jokes and he rebuked
me sharply once for telling one. He did enjoy good pornography, however, and wanted to be told about good pornographic
books. I felt that he had a kind of reverent attitude toward the
female body and vagina as well as toward the phallus.

That his sadism was a desperate attempt to reach someone
deeply, to break the "skin barrier," is clear. It is the mad endeavor somehow to really touch or reach a person's inner being,
to make a union of oneself with the other, to erase all distances.
When conventional methods do not achieve this, perhaps pain
will do it—so may run the sadist's feeling. When Paulus could

---

her, it would be better, because then I would know she did not leave me of her
own free will." Thus the child develops a strain of killing behavior, i.e., sadism.

make a relationship which was profound and loving, he did not need the paraphernalia of sadism. Several women, who are my friends, loved him and he them. With them there was no sadism at all on his part. It seemed that when he was sure of a woman's relationship to him, when he touched reality authentically and on its deepest levels, that was all he wanted; he was satisfied.

His guilt came out in wholesale fashion. His fantasies were often about judges and criminals. Through torture the guilty person would be made to confess. These fantasies were kept up by letter in serial fashion with certain women who would play the game with him. In punishing the criminal in these "serials" he surely was punishing himself. Some of this great guilt, I hypothesize, was related to his having won his mother away from his father. Some of it was due to his recognition of his need for revenge on his mother. Some of it was from his inner reaction to his own sadistic tendencies.

Paulus carried considerable tension about the guilt and other difficulties these erotic patterns brought upon him. To understand it we must imagine ourselves back in the thirties and forties and consider the prejudices of his profession and our culture at that time. In his letters there is no proud boastfulness. There is guilt, and also his serious questions about love, his pondering, and his nonconformist practice. At one time a woman who loved him and whom he loved wrote him about love, and Paulus answered that she had given him an excellent anatomy of it, more convincingly logical than his own view. In her description, he wrote,

[Love] has become an independent principle, not bound by the necessities of its social and economic implications. . . . The fact that a human being (who is a female) as you makes this step, gives me more courage in this respect than even the most valid arguments, and your arguments are certainly valid. How I thank you! My only hope is that I never violated too much the principle of agape which transcends even the anatomy of love.

He carried his actions deeply on his conscience, as is shown in another letter to this person. Thanking her for writing, which was "balm for my soul," he continues,

My soul is hurt because a dear friend's soul is hurt, and I identify myself with him inescapably. . . . [He] is accused—with much justification on the factual side—of erotic misbehavior. He must and is willing to bear the consequences. When I was told about it, it produced a tremendous earthquake in my whole being. I saw myself as I would be seen by others. Was my way right? I dared much (as you did) internally. Daring includes the possibility, and often the probability, of failure. Was my erotic life a failure or was it a daring way of opening up new human possibilities? I do not know the answer. But I am more inclined to give a self-rejecting than a self-affirming answer. In any case, neither my soul nor my body are able to continue the old line in this state of my being. No arguments for or against will do now. But your presence in letter or reality does do! Give it to me fully.

In deepest love,

P.

The last two sentences restate his basic needs and are an important demonstration of his yearning for intimacy. But the crux of the letter is that sentence, "Was my erotic life a failure, or was it a daring way of opening up new human possibilities?"

I have no hesitation in stating my own conclusion: it was clearly the latter. Given the Victorian age out of which he came and the Weimar Republic in which he matured, his was by and large a courageous pilgrimage on another frontier. We do not need to accept his specific forms of behavior in love or marriage. But he ventured greatly and was greatly rewarded, despite all the difficulties he so keenly felt in his own heart. With a few exceptions, I have rarely met a woman who knew him who did not prize and treasure the experience.

In our 1960s and 1970s, Paulus' eroticism would be accepted without much of a stir. In this sense, with all his problems in loving, he was perhaps three decades ahead of his time. Under all the social and ritualistic and economic questions, he continually struggled with the basic question about love: Is the love authentic? Authentic as an emotion, but also as a commitment of being?

CHAPTER 6

The Agony
of Doubt

Tillich loved the "experience of the abyss," or what he also called the "holy void." We saw in his early poem, where he uses "abyss" in its negative sense, indicating his fear of it; we see later, when it is used positively, his liking for it.

These terms refer to Dantean realms of semidarkness filled with chaos cloaked in mist and vapor, but—and this was most important—a chaos crying, like clay on the sculptor's bench, to be made into form. It is against the background of Paulus' childhood experiences in his village, in which the stone walls and gates spoke to him of ancient legends, that his liking for such terms as "abyss" and "holy void" must be understood.

They are an expression of his decisive mysticism. He himself finds the roots of this in the German mystics like Jacob Boehme, and influenced by such thinkers as Schelling and Nietzsche. From this element his rational concepts and principles derived much strength. For the mysticism gave a cosmic base to his rationality, and it also ensured that his reason would always be open-ended, always ready to recognize new possibilities.

Anyone who has practiced meditation will be familiar with what Paulus meant by this experience of the abyss. His capacity for it began in childhood and developed powerfully in the years from fourteen to seventeen, when he tells us the creations of his own imagination were more real to him—and he took them more seriously—than the external world of reality. As he wrote of this in mature life, he was entirely aware of the dangers: too great a withdrawal, lack of contact with other minds, and, as we would call it today, the lure of idiosyncratic thinking.

But his fertile imagination was also an outlet for his already remarkable mind. It cultivated his sense of play and fantasy, which were always so endearing in Paulus. It opened his mind and spirit to the later influence of modern art. Indeed it made him so sensitive to art in its various forms that, encyclopedic as his learning was, he would still read the meaning of a historical period not in assembled data but in its typical works of art. The ecstasy which he was later to know in looking at the mosaics at Ravenna owed something to this early development of imagination. He depended in later life on his insight into the meaning of art; which required courage. I recall when he wrote an address for the opening of the new wing of the Modern Museum in New York. Entitled "The Art of No Art," it was a discussion of pop art and op-art, which he believed were transitional movements in contrast to lasting ones, or as the title proposes, the "art of no art."

At the crucial age when his mother died of her painful cancer, this introverted imagination in which he had dangerously lived among his fantasies was transformed into philosophical imagination. This gave him the necessary logical control and perspective, but still permitted the full range of imaginative scope. One of Paulus' greatest attractions to his friends and greatest aids in speaking and writing was this very active imagination: he saw unique and original aspects of any problem and grasped relationships which no one else could see before he pointed them out. When I pick up a piece of his writing I can be sure that under its Germanisms I will find soaring ideas that are convincing not only because of their logic but also because they perform a kind of "deep calling unto deep" in my own imagination.

This is one of the reasons his ideas are so fecund; they invariably incite the listener to new thought of his own. At his lectures, I would often be so captivated by some thought of his that my own mind would go galloping off in different directions; I would be chagrined to find that before I could get it lassoed and brought back I had missed the next point in the lecture. I was even glad at times that he did stumble over words and ask his audience's help in finding them—at least it gave me a pause in which to follow up some thought he had inspired. His ideas always opened doors to new possibilities. I had the feeling that a new world was lying beyond the gray area at the edge of my mind, a world of wisdom and joy as well as sensuousness, and I longed to live in it.

The experience of the abyss, he believed, "transcends values."[1] Though he had bought the *Critique of Pure Reason* and read it avidly as a young man, he never could fully accept Kantianism or Neo-Kantianism; they were too immediately ethical, the moral imperative was too quickly present. They took away the experience of the abyss. If you leap too quickly to the ethical principle, he believed, you will miss the richness of the experience. The abyss is a realm of creative chaos which transcends values. It is transmoral—prior to the ethical. It does not surprise us when he names Nietzsche as the philosopher who most clearly expresses it.

Hence he had a preference for Romanesque churches with their dark, dank corners where only a faint light filters through —a mystic illumination which conjures up the sense of the abyss and the holy void. This gave Paulus the feeling of a mysterious presence in which he could directly experience himself.

1. *The Interpretation of History* (New York: Charles Scribner's Sons, 1936), p. 36.

It also fits his liking for gray days. Visiting us in New Hampshire, he appreciated the misty, partly overcast character of the day when we went sailing, and when he afterward lay on top of Rattlesnake Mountain looking down at the soft outlines of islands in the lake. This preference presumably went all the way back to his childhood summers on the Baltic Sea, a locality not noted for its sunshine. Late in life he wrote a letter to a friend which recounted some malady of his, and added, "One of the reasons for the nervous strain (the most external one) is the uninterrupted bright sun and lack of rain for seven weeks. I need sometimes the envelopment by clouds and fog and rain. Too much ultraviolet is bad for the organism."

Now a cloudy, overcast, or stormy sky invites visual penetration. There is a seduction in the storminess; as in a Tobey painting, you are aware of realm after realm behind the surface if you have the courage to look further. To what kind of Witch's Sabbath does it lead? One can understand the idea in children's fairy tales of the hero being lured into the forest simply because it is dark and gray—and thus enticing.

On the Rorschach test the gray responses, so often called clouds in various forms, are generally an indication of anxiety. But this must be qualified: they are also the response of creative persons who can tolerate more uncertainty, who love unresolved forms and can accept the anxiety that goes with chaotic states. Such persons can hold on to nonsensical fragments in the mind which they have a suspicion mean something, until such time as they do become more than fragments. In Frank Barron's studies of the difference between people who were not particularly creative and those whose accomplishments had proven their creativity, the former almost always selected the orderly cards while the latter expressed a clear preference for the chaotic cards. This helps us understand Paulus' love of uncertainty, and it also shows the relation between his creativity and his doubts.

Not that he did not experience anxiety. Living with *Angst*, as it is called in his mother tongue, is part of the price of loving the abyss. Tillich believed that anxiety was the subjective side of the tension between being and nonbeing in a sense similar to Heidegger's, and that it was therefore inevitable. The *Angst* could attach itself to almost anything in his existence. In a letter to a friend while he was on board ship going to Europe, he writes,

I could and could not sleep, was full of anxiety about everything in the next days, heard all the noises of our nightly stopping at Cobh, had terrible dreams about Hannah and the whole family, took Seconal (for the first time) and awoke in rain and cold but with your letter. . . . I started working on the Hamburg lectures. These are about the same subject as the Yale lectures (you remember my discontent) and the third volume[2] (you remember my worries last summer). I am worried more than ever. The system crumbles. What shall I do? Shall I collect fragments? Declare that the attempt failed? Try it again—which I probably will do. . . . It is all as I experienced it when I was 12 years old: the whip of anxiety about unfinished work! I kiss thee in despairing passion.

But this penchant for *Angst* and for doubting had within its remarkably positive motives. It was as though Paulus set up various hypotheses, agonized with them, saw which fit and which did not and how they could be ordered. In an age when people are grasping for whatever they can find to believe, when multitudes call for reassurance and security at any price, he chose to doubt. "Sometimes I think it is my mission to bring faith to the faithless, and doubt to the faithful," he wrote. He doubted not as an intellectual method, as Descartes had done. Doubt, for Paulus, was rather an unavoidable characteristic of our transitional age and an inescapable concomitant of his creativity.

"Orthodoxy is intellectual pharisaism," he said. As his student

2. Of his *Systematic Theology.*

this sentence meant for me a proof of his honesty. I knew the uncertainty, the doubting, did not represent intellectual sparring, but came out of the agony and the struggles of a first-class mind authentically searching. This yielded the freshness and frankness for which, in my teachers, I so longed.

2

Paulus' love of the abyss was connected with his choice of living always "on the boundary." This phrase, which is his own, is well chosen: it does not mean, here, a point remote or on the mere edge of any area of life, but the line of encounter between opposing forces—a position in which you are vulnerable to shots from both sides. Someone has to mediate, to make a connection through his own life between opposites. Paulus not only chose this for himself but was chosen for it by his fate, as demonstrated in his exile. He lived perpetually on the tense and delicate borders of the world, on the frontiers of thought and experience. That, he said, was the most "propititous place for acquiring knowledge."

The line between conscious and unconscious experience—a thin one—is an example of the boundary as a place where people's inner lives are opened and their generally private thoughts become spoken. His taking me by the arm and saying, "Now tell me what you *really* think" was an example of his invitation to everyone he had contact with to live on that boundary with him. His colleague and friend Reinhold Niebuhr said once in describing Tillich, "He is trying to walk a fence between man's doubts and the traditions of man's faith. He walks the fence with great virtuosity, and if he slips a bit to one side or the other, it is hardly noticed by us humble pedestrians."

There was, first, the political boundary: he was an exile. In no example can we see more clearly the fact that a man's choices can complement his destiny. He was exiled radically against his desires, he came to this country as an exile, chose it "in spite of," and resigned himself to a truncated life in his new land. But he found, much to his surprise, that the transplanting was valuable and in some mysterious metaphysical way necessary for his further development.

There was also the boundary between philosophy and theology. Paulus is the only modern thinker I know who follows that combination with equal care for each discipline. Once an entire meeting of the America Philosophical Association was given over to a discussion of his philosophy, which bespeaks the eminence his colleagues accorded him.

Much criticism has been leveled at Tillich for this riding of two horses, especially from the Barthian wing which makes a radical separation between the two. But for Paulus these two disciplines, although distinguishable, were inseparable. He is a philosopher so far as clarifying the questions of man is concerned: hearing and seeing clearly the problems posed by man's limitations, and his striving for the infinite. These inquiries fall in the realm of philosophy. But the answers—such as creation, the concept of God, the spirit, Christ, the kingdom— belong in the field of theology

He also lived on the boundary between the intellectuals and the proletariat, which he called the border between Karl Marx and the middle class. He was always aware of the class barrier (more rigid in Germany than in this country) and carried his share of guilt for his position in it. "My belonging to the privileged class," he writes, "early aroused in me that consciousness of social guilt which later was to become of such decisive importance for my work and the course of my life."[3]

When Tillich spoke on Sunday mornings in the chapel at Union Seminary, a motley crowd overflowed the main auditorium and balcony. In contrast to the white collars and banker-

3. *The Interpretation of History*, p. 9.

like gray mien of most church congregations, this audience was colorful to say the least: blue collars, open collars, and sometimes no collars at all. Many had long hair; a good many were German exiles—flamboyant persons from the intellectual or art worlds who probably went to church only when Tillich was speaking. After the service, the usual coterie of women surrounded him, each one of whom no doubt felt the sermon was an intimate personal message to her. The titles of the sermons themselves lead one to ponder: "Loneliness and Solitude," "The Eternal Now," "Heal the Sick; Cast Out Demons," "On the Transitoriness of Life," or "Meditation: The Mystery of Time."

After the service we would go to some local residence where we would drink sherry and Paulus would eagerly ask for criticisms of his speech. There would then be what he loved, an inspired discussion. His friends were colorful in a different sense: at a Tillich party I would meet such persons as W. H. Auden, Bertolt Brecht, and Karen Horney.

There was also the boundary between what Paulus called heteronomy and autonomy. "I am determined to stand on the border of autonomy and heteronomy . . . even if the coming period of human history should stand under the emblem of heteronomy."[4] Well, it does stand under that emblem: we are in the period of conformism and polytheism, a time when a vast maelstrom of things happens without apparent central guiding principles.

Paulus chose autonomy, but again at a price. He could understand the heteronomy; indeed he lived within it, while at the same time could see it in a perspective. Thus he was not overwhelmed by the tendency to mistake it for a vague pluralism. He asked always, What are the underlying assumptions on which such a heteronomy is based? In this sense he was an

4. Ibid., p. 30.

authentic part of our culture. But holding to an autonomous position in a heteronomous culture is difficult indeed.

Part of the price he had to pay was *guilt*. Most of all it was guilt at pushing through to autonomous ideas. "The immemorial experience of mankind, that new knowledge can be won only through breaking a taboo, that all autonomous thinking is accompanied by a consciousness of guilt, has been the fundamental experience of my own life."[5] This, from one side, is the age-old paradox of creativity. Here we have the myth of Prometheus, who having stolen fire from the gods and given it to mankind is then punished by Zeus: chained to a rock in the Caucasus mountains to have his liver eaten daily by vultures. Adam and Eve illustrate another breaking of a taboo, interpreted in Genesis as a rebellion against God, for which they also are punished. These are projections in myth of the universal experience of mankind, though expressed in different ways and related to multifarious elements in the individual's life history. Paulus was keenly aware of the consequent guilt.

He felt that guilt is "existentially universal," a part of every person's existence which begins with the infant's birth. He believed, along with Kierkegaard, that such guilt can be used as inspiration for new creativity, and I think his life demonstrates the fact.

I found this awareness of guilt in Tillich a great relief. Most Americans, I had observed, pride themselves on perpetually smiling, feeling "great" when they get up in the morning ready to "live out their potentialities" for the new day. This masks in most of them an endemic depression, reflected not only in the consumption of great quantities of pills, but also motivating its opposite. the violence which is so prevalent, covertly and overtly, in our society. At the least, it seems an emotionally dishonest way of encountering the world. I knew that *I*, in any

5. Ibid., p. 23.

case, was not this everlastingly cheerful creature.

There was none of this pretense in Paulus. When someone on the elevator in the morning would ask him how he was, he would respond with a catalog of his miseries, unaware that the person was asking as a mere formality and was not really interested. "Every morning from seven till ten I live with the demons," he remarked.[6] True, he extracted at times some extra mileage out of parading his miseries—friends then excusing him more readily from their excessive demands on his time. It is interesting that those of us who knew him well had no difficulty in distinguishing between miseries used as a protection in Paulus and his authentic guilt feeling.

The origins of this "existentially universal" guilt are shown in an eloquent lecture he gave in Germany shortly before his death. He was speaking of those Germans during World War II, who, helpless to do anything, had suppressed their knowledge of the Nazi persecution of the Jews.

We do not condemn them, for we all suppress things we cannot bear to know. *What man of even the slightest sensitivity, can look at himself in a mirror?* One looks away from one's own reflection. This is the psychological mechanism about which I am talking. One should not deny this mechanism either in himself or in others.[7]

It is impossible, Paulus also believed, to have a sensitive and a good conscience at the same time. From this awareness of guilt came one of the most appealing and human aspects of his speaking and writing, namely that he always included himself in the human frailties to which he referred.

6. I have elsewhere noted that this was quoted to me by a schizophrenic woman who had gone to Tillich complaining of *her* demons. His statement helped her immensely, keeping her psychological balance for the time being. If he lived with the demons, she could also endure it. The remark bridged her isolation, welcoming her back ito the community of the human race.

7. "The Jewish Question: Christian and German Problem," *Jewish Social Studies*, 33 (October 1971): 255. Italics mine.

True, he was often depressed. It was a general motif running through his life, expressed in his emphasis on physical miseries, in his feeling continually overworked, and in his constant worry about not doing his work well enough. He sometimes impressed people as a man beset by life.

There are two things to be said about his depressions. Some of his appearance of depression was really a *mode de parler;* perhaps this had its source in the age-old strategy of warding off the envy of the gods. But the other and more important thing was that his depressions never made the rest of us depressed. It is the *repressed* depression, the pretense, the cover-up of depression that communicates itself to those around a person. We are more apt to feel depressed by the perpetually smiling individual than the one who is honestly sad. If we admit our depression openly and freely, those around us get from it an experience of freedom rather than the depression itself. And this is how it was with Paulus.

Nevertheless, there was a great deal of depression in his life which had psychological rather than existential roots. To understand this we need to consider, albeit briefly, his relation with his father.

3

Paulus speaks of his father as a "conscientious, very dignified, completely convinced and, in the presence of doubt, angry supporter of the conservative Lutheran point of view."[8] He writes of the long and penetrating philosophical discussions he had with his father almost nightly when he was a boy:

In the tradition of classical orthodoxy my father loved and used philosophy, convinced that there can be no conflict between a true philosophy and revealed truth. The long philosophical discussions which de-

8. *The Theology of Paul Tillich,* paperback, ed. by Charles W. Kegley and Robert W. Bretall (New York: The MacMillan Company, 1961), p. 8.

veloped belong to the most happy instances of a positive relation to my father. Nevertheless, in these discussions the break-through occurred. From an independent philosophical position a state of independence spread out into all directions, theoretically first, practically later. It is this difficult and painful break-through to autonomy which has made me immune to any system of thought or life which demands the surrender of this autonomy."[9]

Paulus took pleasure in the memories of his father teaching him to sail. One evening in 1950 at a New Year's Eve party at the Tillich apartment he made his usual speech—this time, since it was mid-century, of reminiscences of a half-century earlier. When he came to tell of his father's taking him to the town hall on New Year's Eve of the year 1900, so great was his emotion that he burst into tears. Sitting there, I marveled at his deep feelings, realizing that we Americans would never cry in public in that way. I envied and valued it, no matter what such emotionalism might be called.

In his twenties he seems to have taken a protective attitude toward this parent. Once when Hannah and her sister M.L. were accompanying his father and himself on a walk in a neighboring town, the two women contradicted the father, who promptly—so M.L. tells me—fell to the ground. Paulus' spontaneous response was a motherly cry of "Vaterkin! Vaterkin!"

But the father was also tyrannical, competitive, and jealous of this son who showed such remarkable promise. He was enraged when Paulus, now launched on his academic career, received an honorary degree from a university before he had received one. The son felt this competition keenly; it was the subject of many dreams and nightmares. A recurring dream in his young manhood was: "I had climbed to the top of the tree. I screamed when my father's arm reached for me and grabbed me to pull me down."

9. Ibid. p. 8.

With respect to competition with his father, if I may put the matter metaphorically, Paulus had won the Oedipal conflict. But it is still impossible not to regard the German father as a formidable figure. In this case he seems to have fulfilled the stereotype of the partially castrated male who pretends to be the titular ruler but knows underneath the pretense that his wife is really the dominant power in the family.

In the course of one of Paulus' quasi-psychoanalytic sessions, he came running out of the room terribly frightened by the fantasy that his father was a snake. This fits the "guiding fiction"[10] we have already seen in Paulus, who, when he was a little boy, may well have experienced his father as a divisive force, the slithering creature who crawled between him and his mother—the phallic form of a diabolic power which sought to tear him from her.

We have seen that Paulus' later battle against narrow doctrine must be understood against the background of his father's orthodox theology. Another phenomenon in later life comes to mind: his inveterate habit, noted earlier, when on vacation by the North Sea, of making as high a pile of sand as he could and then sitting on top of it. Was this king-of-the-castle position still an acting out of the Oedipal struggle with his father?

These sketches of Paulus' relation with his father are enough to indicate the roots of difficult and lasting problems.

4

Tillich obviously had to have some way of dealing with the problems of his *Angst*, his guilt, and his relation with his father. His philosophy served him as a source of courage *(Courage to Be)* and also as a way of rationalizing those difficulties he could not control. Freud to the contrary, this does not necessarily make his philosophy a reaction formation, any more than it

10. An Adlerian term for the personal myth by which each of us lives.

makes Freud's psychoanalysis a reaction formation. The validity of a method has to be judged on its own merits.

One of Tillich's problems was that bringing his sense of logic and his emotions into some kind of accord. This was hard, and he did not greatly succeed. I used to say to him that, while his mind had developed magnificently, his emotions had been left behind at the twelve-year-old level. He never denied it. He generally accepted it as food for thought (hence to be taken care of by rational means!).

His categories were necessary to control his Dionysian emotions. When he was emotionally involved and did not wish at that moment to work the involvement through, apparently his logic would come in to protect him. I wrote him once asking why Mephistopheles in Goethe's *Faust* came to collect the latter's soul at exactly the moment when Faust was at last experiencing some contentment about life.[11] He answered (through a letter from Hannah) that it was because that was the agreement in their original contract. Now this is an entirely logical answer, but tells me nothing I did not already know. What I wanted to know was the psychological and mythological reasons that made Goethe himself portray them as putting it in the contract.

I have believed since then that Paulus had an identification with Faust that deeply involved his emotions. Both were devoted to the power of knowledge. Both were giants (I often find myself thinking that Paulus was the last of the individual giants of our historical era). Both experienced a great deal of sensuality along the way; we have seen this in Paulus' life, and his guilt

11. The lines from *Faust*, in translation, are:

> Then dared I hail the moment fleeing:
> "*Ah, linger—thou art so fair!*
> The traces cannot, of mine earthly being,
> In aeons perish—they are there!—
> In proud fore-feeling of such lofty bliss,
> I now enjoy the highest Moment—this!"

about it. He often acted, indeed, as though he had sold his soul to Mephistopheles, a guilt he consciously admitted. In such avowals, I suggest, his logic came to the rescue and protection of his undeveloped emotional involvement.

Paulus began his thinking always with people—their questions, their being, their predicament. This is another source of his identification with all human frailty. Of man he wrote, "In his own existence he has the only possible approach to existence itself." Elsewhere he writes that "the principles which constitute the universe must be sought in man," and the converse holds, that what is found in man's experience is to some extent a reflection of what is true in the universe.[12]

This is the source of his famous method of "correlation." Existential man's questions on one side are correlated with the theological answers on the other. Put religiously, God does not answer questions that are not first asked. To be sure, the fact that man can ask given questions is partially related to his previous religious experience. Out of this comes the special way Tillich unites his philosophy and theology. The former has to do with the questions, the clarification of them, elaborating their ramifications, and so on, the latter has to do with the theological endeavors to answer. The concluding sentence in the preface to his seminal book, *Systematic Theology*, makes this clear, "A help in answering questions: this is exactly the purpose of this theological system."[13] Thus the titles of its parts are: "Reason and Revelation," "Being and God," "Existence and the Christ," "Life and the Spirit," and "History and the Kingdom of God."

12. Alexander McKelway is correct when he writes:

Tillich is a philosophic anomaly. Philosophers today have for the most part confined themselves either to an introspective, subjective analysis of existence and steadfastly refused to abstract universals, or they have confined themselves to those concepts which are open to verification and proof. Against both of these lines, but combining aspects of both, Paul Tillich vigorously asserts the classical and medieval doctrine of ontology. (*The Systematic Theology of Paul Tillich* [New York: Delta Books, 1964]).

13. *Systematic Theology* (Chicago: University of Chicago Press, 1951), 1:xii.

This method earned for him, again, a good deal of criticism, particularly from the Barthians. They believe with Calvin that the order in the method should be: first God, then man. For Tillich, man in his questioning is the beginning, then God. Though he often soared high in his writing about spirit, he always identified himself with man as his basis.

But in another highly constructive fashion his philosophy proposes a way for all men and women—regardless of idiosyncratic problems—to deal with their lives. I refer to his important emphasis on courage.

Courage—coming from the Latin *cor* and the French *coeur*, meaning heart—is here restored to philosophy, indeed, given an ontological importance. He believed that courage was essential to the experience of meaning in life. It is not merely one virtue among others, but the fundamental virtue upon which all others depend. Like the heart which vitalizes all the other organs in the body by pumping blood to them, courage gives power to all the other virtues. The self-affirmation of being—the essential meaning of courage—is against threats of nonbeing such as illness, loneliness, or intellectual limitations. Courage is both ontological, i.e., having its source in being as such, and also moral, i.e., the source of right relations with others. The basis for this self-affirmation is the ground of being and meaning, which in Paulus' sense is God.

No one experiences the values of life, whether knowledge or joy or beauty, by passively waiting for them to come to him. As though being born were a guarantee of one's automatic achievement of these values! Human values have to be confronted, labored for, earned. Their existence depends upon our courage.

This is why *The Courage To Be* is such an important book and such a valuable source for Tillich's theology.[14] I have always

14. Paperback ed., New Haven: Yale University Press, 1959.

spoken of it as the most existential book written in America. For Paulus, courage is the self-affirmation of being in spite of nonbeing.[15] Here we have the secret of his attitude toward anxiety, guilt, and depression, all of which can in some of their forms be expressions of nonbeing. We see now why he never tried to repress them but met them head on.

Life always consists of affirmation *in spite of.* Like a thoroughbred racehorse, he gloried in the tension this produced. Those who remark disapprovingly that Paulus was a "troubled man" are correct in their description—who among us would not be anxious and guilty and depressed if he were to face his life openly? But they are wrong in their condemnation of him for not putting on a better front. On the flyleaf of the copy of *The Courage to Be* which he gave me, Paulus wrote as a motto the sentence from the book quoted earlier: "The self is the stronger the more non-being it can take into itself." Thus if we can accept normal anxiety and guilt, if we can live with our anger, we become the stronger; but we also find, as in the psychotherapeutic confronting of anger, that feelings of love also increase. The anxiety turns out to be not so unbearable after all, and our pretense in trying to repress it simply a way of cutting off our experience of life.

As I lay in bed at Saranac Lake for two years with tuberculosis, I often thought of Paulus, though I did not see him. It is too simple to say he was a model for me. *The Courage to Be* had yet to be written, eight years later. But I did remember his fortitude in all the blows life had dealt him: World War I, his first divorce, his anxiety and loneliness, his confrontation with Hitler, his emigration and exile. And I recalled how he had met them all with courage and turned them to constructive use. Then my resentment against life for visiting me with the sinis-

15. Ibid., p. 172.

ter bacilli, my feeling of morbid self-pity that I had had such a hard time of it, were laid bare as the superficial complaints they were. I saw that no one can directly and successfully combat his destiny, but each of us, by virtue of the small margin of freedom that prevails even in a sanatorium bed, can choose his attitude *toward* that destiny. Shall it be servile abdication or some form of courage? If the latter, we may well find that we have formed and molded our own fate. This is human freedom.

The "courage to accept acceptance," which is the theme of the last chapter of Tillich's book, is a superb peroration. We are not simply isolated selves, he points out; we are interdependent on and with each other. The acceptance by significant persons —and for the religious person, by God—is essential to our acceptance of ourselves. But amazingly enough, it is very difficult, and was especially so for Paulus. When a woman he loved wrote him reassuring him of her own and the world's acceptance of him, he did not deny what she wrote. But he answered, "Yes, I have produced the phrase, 'You are accepted.' But I can never say it to *me*. Bach can and you can. And Bach can only if you can. For you are alive and warm and near."

It needed the human touch and human love, someone who was alive and warm and near. This is the man who had such zest for life. He is the man who loved men and women and good food and wine. He is the man who experienced pervasive joy *in spite of* and *because of* his anxiety, uncertainty, and depression. He is like Beethoven—deaf and with plenty of miseries, writing the *Ode to Joy*. Paulus is the one man I have known who could write the following paragraph:

> The affirmation of one's essential being in spite of desires and anxieties creates joy. Lucillus is exhorted by Seneca to make it his business "to learn how to feel joy." It is not the joy of fulfilled desires to which he refers, for real joy is a "severe matter"; it is the happiness of a soul which is "lifted above every circumstance." Joy accompanies the self-affirmation of our essential being in spite of the inhibitions coming

from the accidental elements in us. Joy is the emotional expression of
the courageous Yes to one's own true being.[16]

When a dear friend of ours—Paulus' and mine—was critically
ill in the hospital and seemed to have spiritually and psychologically given up, he went regularly to see her. "Helen," he said
to her, "You must *love* life." He was certainly not nondirective,
but it worked. He communicated to her not only an attitude
toward life but life itself.

16. Ibid., p. 14.

CHAPTER 7

That God
Beyond God

In one of the books about Tillich's ideas there is a chapter entitled "Is Paul Tillich a dangerous man?"[1] His answer to this question, also quoted in the volume, was characteristically a short Yes, given with his endearing smile. In another place theologian Nels F. S. Ferré held that Tillich was "the most dangerous theological leader alive."[2] Though I am not writing primarily about Paulus' ideas but about himself, there are points where the two are intertwined beyond separation, and this is one of them. When I was a student these attacks upon him gave me occasion for a good deal of thought.

The substance of them was mainly to the effect that Paulus was an atheist. He had said often in class, and wrote it in many places as well as in his magnum opus: "God does not exist. He is being itself beyond essence and existence. Therefore to argue that God exists is to deny him."[3]

1. *Ultimate Concern: Tillich in Dialogue,* ed. by D. M. Brown (New York: Harper & Row, 1965), p. 188.
2. Those who wish to read Nels F. S. Ferré's view can do so in his chapter in *The Theology of Paul Tillich,* ed. by Charles W. Kegley and Robert W. Bretall (New York: The Macmillan Company, 1952), pp. 248–268.
3. Quoted in *Systematic Theology,* p. 205; also in Alexander McKelway, *The Systematic Theology of Paul Tillich* (New York: Delta Books, 1964), p. 118.

I knew what he meant—that God cannot be a being beside other beings. If he is existence, he cannot be essence. To insist that he is a being "above" or "below" all others still makes him a being apart from other beings, some "greatest being" we posit in the universe existing among the stars. If he is a thing, some other things in the universe must be outside his control, and he must be subject to the structure as a whole. A whole hornet's nest of absurd problems is opened up, such as the question, "How did God spend his time before he created the earth?" Paulus told us once the answer for that given by his students in Germany: "Thinking up punishments for those who ask such questions."

I had often heard from Paulus himself the convincing reasons he had for insisting on this point. Some of these are given in his writings.

For God as a subject makes me into an object which is nothing more than an object. He deprives me of my subjectivity because he is all-powerful and all-knowing. I revolt and try to make *him* into an object, but the revolt fails and becomes desperate. God appears as the invincible tyrant, the being in contrast with whom all other beings are without freedom and subjectivity. He is equated with the recent tyrants who with the help of terror try to transform everything into a mere object, a thing among things, a cog in the machine they control. He becomes the model of everything against which Existentialism revolted. This is the God Nietzsche said had to be killed because nobody can tolerate being made into a mere object of absolute knowledge and absolute control.[4]

Recalling Tillich's experience with the tyrants in contemporary Europe, I could well empathize with him.

God, rather, is *being itself,* the ground of meaning and being. This does not make Paulus a pantheist; the meaning is not found merely in nature, nor in other "things." He valued mysticism as it is found in persons close to nature, and he valued intuition.

4. *The Courage to Be,* paperback ed. (New Haven: Yale University Press, 1959), p. 185.

But he also greatly valued reason, and it was the logical fallacy in the idea of God's existence that upset him most.

I was keenly aware that every great thinker who dares to push ahead on the frontier, who upsets the inherited beliefs of conventional people, is attacked in similar ways. This put Paulus in the company of Spinoza, the "God-intoxicated philosopher" who was excommunicated as an atheist. All my adult life I had been thrilled whenever I recalled the picture of Socrates being condemned to death by the good Athenian citizens for teaching "false daimonia," or false gods, to the youth of Athens. In the *Apologia* he answers his accusers at his trial with the statement, "I do believe in the gods and in a sense deeper than my accusers." Paulus could have said as much. Indeed, a similar attack was leveled against Jesus himself. Paulus was indeed in distinguished company.

I want here, however, to describe my feelings as a student when I heard his statements. A wave of freedom swept over me —freedom from all the futile arguments of undergraduate days. *The Christian Century* had run a series of debates among Henry Wieman, a naturalistic "theist" of the University of Chicago; Rudolph Otto, an "atheist" at the University of Wisconsin; and some theologian whose name escapes me, on the question, "Is There a God?" The debates got no place at all. Even as an undergraduate I could see that all such debates were doomed before they started. I was later to observe that the trouble was in this little article "*a* God." Even such a sophisticated critic as Michael Novak, in a piece on Paulus in *Commentary*, slides into the same error when he speaks of "*a* God" from time to time.[5] I was freed from all that useless controversy.

I felt freed also from the nagging inner *compulsion to believe.* Carried over from childhood, intellectually superseded but still present in some deep corner of my emotions, some compulsion

5. "The Religion of Paul Tillich," *Commentary* 43 (April 1967): 56.

pushed me to believe this or that because my mother and father
had believed it. The main trouble with the drive to believe is
that it sets up exactly the opposite compulsion: to disbelieve. To
throw a bomb into the parents' "faith" (which in many cases was
no great faith anyway, but chiefly a deep sense of the importance of not smoking or drinking alcohol or swearing). I was
here subject to a childish form of what Nietzsche proclaimed,
the great eye of God which nobody can stand peering at him
all the time.

But as I heard Paulus expound these ideas, I also felt a wave
of anxiety at the same time. It was partly the disturbance that
always comes with freedom—the "dizziness" of freedom, as
Kierkegaard put it. And it was also partly that Paulus' statement
took away *my* security, that childish belief to which, against all
intellectual development, I apparently still clung. I knew that
God for most people was the guarantor of the status quo; he
protected them from fundamental upset, from moral anarchy.
God guarded the sanctity of marriage, he was against crime, he
protected property (especially if you belonged to one of the
sects that sprang from Calvinism).

The word "atheist" conjured up all the opposite things: a
satanic person who is antimoral, who believes in free love, who
is dishonest and would torture your grandmother, plus all the
invective hurled at "atheistic communism" in our day. Infantile
as were these vestigial remnants of my early imprinting, and
outrageous to my reason as they still are, I cannot deny that they
existed some where in my consciousness. It required not logic
but living, and time, to mature beyond such superstitions. It also
required living and time to absorb what Paulus was trying to
say.

Paulus believed in the "God above God" as the chapter head-
ing in one of his books phrases it.[6] To me this means that man's

6. *The Courage to Be*, op. cit., p. 186.

concept of God is continually changing; it is flexible, dynamic, always "in process." But paradoxically, it is at the same time an apprehension of the eternal. Linear reasoning is powerless to express this paradox. But the phrase "God above God," does express the eternal in a metaphor which does not crystallize into dogma.

2

The flaw in Tillich's system is claimed by Alexander McKelway, who is a Barthian, to be as follows:

The problem and danger [of Tillich], to put the matter simply, is the lack of a consistent focus on the revelation of God in Jesus Christ. In the doctrines of man and Christ which we have reviewed, there is the danger that man will be seen apart from who he is revealed to be in Christ, and that God's revelation and salvation will be found in some other way or at some other place than in Jesus Christ. Christian theology bases its knowledge of God entirely on his self-revelation in Jesus Christ.[7]

When I read this statement, I found myself expostulating, "So much the better for Paulus!" I, for one, have little patience

7. Karl Barth, the most influential theologian of our day, is one whose thought does meet the emotional needs of many people in our age of anxiety and alienation and almost total lack of security. I was told on good authority that Karl Barth, when he was tried by the Nazis, read from a book before the court. This book was Socrates' *Apologia*, quoted above. So Barth's position on *life* does not omit entirely the cultural side, though it seems to in his theology.

Tillich remains, and would always remain in his writings, insistent on taking in the riches of culture, with the necessary understanding and necessary distinctions among them, and he finds the theological meaning in them.

Another approach to this problem is to point out that Barthianism came at a time of dissolution of European culture, politically speaking. It gave a point of reference to its adherents which enabled them to face the disasters and the issues of life and death with fortitude, since there was a point outside human life from which to gain perspective. Tillich, on the other hand, accepted the dissolution *itself* into his thought, he saw *meaning* in the dissolution of societies in human history; and he derived revelation from every act of history and every aspect of contemporary culture. He loved it all, sentimental as that sounds; this is what made him so human, and in turn so lovable.

these days for beliefs that serve not to encompass people but to rule them out of the kingdom. I do not deny the necessity, for the sake of reason if nothing else, of distinguishing beliefs. But I believe the challenge of our day is to move away from the divisive world toward new understanding of other worlds and other peoples.

Yes, Paulus *did* find revelation in other ways. He found it in contemporary artists, he found it in movements for justice, he found it in the mountains and the sea, in nature, and in acts of human devotion and love. He would firmly distinguish the degrees of revelation; I am not at all saying he would lump these things all together. But he steadfastly refused to limit the breaking through of transcendent truth to the one revelation in Jesus Christ. I agree with Michael Novak, "Wherever men are ultimately concerned with the most creative human values they can discover, they have in their experience, Tillich would say, pointers to the presence of God."[8]

Do these things mean, as Novak and some others believe, that Tillich will be eclipsed? His language does not seem to meet the modern temper, and will his thought, following his language, fall into disregard? "Tillich sought to heal modern culture, but the culture was uninterested," says Bultmann. Rabbi Richard L. Rubenstein learned of the death of Paulus, who had been his teacher, while visiting the site of the Warsaw ghetto. He wrote of the occasion:

Somehow, there was something appropriate in hearing the sad news in that place. An important part of Tillich's greatness was his ability to endow with theological meaning the universal dissolution in two world wars of the old certainties of European civilization. Tillich had known the stability which preceded the breakdown. He had the courage to confront the breakdown and discern within it possibilities of theological renewal.

8. Op. cit., p. 65.

My sadness was tempered by the knowledge that Tillich's work was, insofar as any man's can be, completed. He had spoken for and to his time, but we have moved beyond that time.[9]

Paulus himself predicted this. Once when I was reassuring him about how he would be read in future generations, he shook his head. "I am determined too much by the present *Kairos*," he said.

Determined by the crisis of his time! Surely every thinker is thus determined. Everyone speaks out of his own time. The real question is, on what level does he find his *Kairos?* Does he penetrate to the depth where particular time is superseded, that level of the archetypes where the eternal myths of history such as Orestes and Oedipus have their existence—the depth where the future as well as the past finds its source? I believe Paulus does reach such a depth.

I want to propose another alternative. It is that Paulus will be temporarily eclipsed, so long as we are in this anxious, alienated age where every man, woman, and child prizes security above all, whether by science or by technical reason or by religious dogma. After that, however, Tillich will be rediscovered and revalued as the thinker who does authentically speak to human beings and their condition.

One of the reasons, I propose, is that his method begins always with the *questions* asked by men, women, and children. We are living in the age of psychology, when man himself has become his own problem. Paulus sensed this and wedded his method to it. He spoke to our culture; and whatever more orthodox thinkers may say, and whether or not the culture listens at any given time, it remains the culture that needs healing.

Another reason is that Paulus gave us a basis for discovering the values we so sorely need. In a day when the young are

9. Ibid.

increasingly and militantly seeking new values, this is important. Paulus did it precisely by *not* focusing on values per se; he never liked the "quest for values" among philosophers. He did it precisely by going below values themselves to their sources in ontology. He asked the question, What does it mean to *be?* Out of the answers to that question came values which do not hang unattached and loose in the air, do not depend upon your digestion for that day, but are essentially and vitally part of our being.

But the third and most important reason of all is: We are moving into a new polytheism.[10] Paulus was the one thinker who saw this and confronted directly and courageously its implications. Our monotheism has become too blatantly allied with destruction. The God of America against the God of communism: these gods war in the swamps of Vietnam, amid indescribable cruelty to children, mangled bodies of adolescent soldiers, and the destruction of a million civilians. Our failure in Vietnam is the ultimate symbol of the demise of the "bombs-for-Allah" kind of faith. The day of the invocation of *Our God* against *Their God* is past—I hope forever. The yellow man has a right to his God as we have a right to ours. The gods of monotheism—of Judaism, Mohammedanism, Christianity—are being superseded whether we like it or not by a new polytheism which is not resurrected from ancient Greece or Israel.

Paulus would have called the new polytheism "heteronomy," meaning many norms, or many pointers in different directions. It is difficult indeed to unify these diverse trends, as he knew only too well. Every culture goes through this "dispersion" at the point of transition between the age that is dying and that which is not yet born. Paulus had predicted in effect our time

10. For a further discussion of the evidence for this polytheism, see David Miller, *Polytheism and Archetypal Theology: A Discussion,* in *Journal of American Academy of Religion,* December 1972, Vol. XL, No. 4, pp. 513–520.

of heteronomy, and had firmly stated that he would stick to autonomy no matter how heteronomous the age became. But my point is that he *understood* the heteronomy. One may recall his profound and remarkable sensitiveness to modern art as one illustration of this. Some parts of it he valued highly; other parts he described as "the art of no art"; but he empathized with the creators of one as of the other. We can be sure he would likewise have understood the polytheism of our culture: the oriental influence through Buddhism, the effort toward community in the communes, the influence of the Old Testament in movements toward racial justice and so on.

As a student of Paulus, I will answer one of the criticisms of him, that the "danger" in his thought is that "salvation will be found in some other way or at some other place than in Jesus Christ." I resoundingly reply, Yes! And who is to say it is not salvation? It is the healing for my spirit, as well as for countless others, and that is what salvation means.

3

Perhaps the most useful way of illustrating the new polytheism will be to give an example of my own meditation. The reader will note that I use in it several different religious strains, coming from varied sources.

When I arrive at my office early in the morning, undisturbed by telephone or traffic, I sit quietly giving my attention first to my dreams of the night before. I analyze them, or at least ponder what the dream is saying to me. This is the *psychoanalytic* aspect of my meditation.

Then I devote ten or fifteen minutes to an "opening" process. I clear my mind as nearly as possible of every content, meditating on nothingness. This, as I experience it, takes me into the deeper levels of being. The haste, the pressures and deadlines that haunt us all in the workaday world drop away; the "machinery" is temporarily halted. The jealousies, resentments and all the mess of backbiting to which human consciousness is heir also tend to evaporate. This experience of being brings with it relief, pleasure, and a very mild ecstasy.

At times my experience of being moves to a deeper dimension in consciousness. I then experience what I can only call Being with a capital *B*. The experience of Being brings a greater ecstasy, a pervasive calmness and sense of beatitude. Anxiety about death, for example, also vanishes: I feel myself part of eternity, part of the Being which was eons of years before I was born and will be eons of years after I die. This is an expression, it seems to me, of "The peace of God which passeth understanding."

This phase of meditation I learned from friends who have spent years in India. Though it has elements of Zen Buddhism, I shall call it the *Hindu* contribution to my meditation.

Third, there is generally some kind of message, some guidance that appears. It comes more readily if I do not stridently *demand* it; if I listen to my "deeper" self, sooner or later it will speak to me. The message which forms itself out of the darkness and the vapor—when one does come—often takes me by surprise. This is generally a sign of its authenticity. This third phase owes a good deal to my *Protestant-Christian* background. It would be surprising if I could cut off my cultural body, nor do I want to. And the Protestant-Christian influence is also present in the images which come to me in my state of receptivity. Sometimes it is the vague form of a heroic-sized man, sometimes a woman, sometimes a moving cauldron of indistinguishable figures, but usually it is the unformed matter before creation permeated with a profound feeling of peace.

Sometimes I meditate on the word and experience of "abyss," and sometimes on the "holy void," both concepts I got from Paulus. I try to keep open in the sense of not getting into any rut, and vary the technique from time to time. I have found that before writing it is best not to go into meditation too deeply: the process of creativity, for me, can work best when I confront an actual chaos, and I do not want too much sense of peace.

This meditation gives me a sense of integration. It aids the process of centering my self. After it, I am more confident of my stance. Whereas before I may have felt like the man who jumped on his horse and galloped off in all directions, I now find these different tendencies coming together into a pattern. As when one travels away from mountains, the foothills decrease in size and the sheer mountains loom higher.

I propose this as an illustration of polytheism used constructively. It is not syncretism nor eclecticism. It is different religions merged into a new gestalt which at this time has meaning and efficacy for me.

Is there in this some hidden pattern, some principle of hierarchy? Do I unconsciously select my Zeus? Is this polytheism merely a *transition* to a new age? Presumably yes. Presumably the polytheism of the present, culturally speaking, has within it a movement toward a new unity. Such a pattern may be discerned in my motive for the selection of these three different "religious" forms. I selected them because in my experience they give me most insight, most expansion. They open up my self and the world around me to my self.

I would choose, therefore, to describe the polytheism as new possibility. It is that which leads to a new *expansion*.

This meditation will perhaps aid the reader, as it does me, to understand Paulus' description of God as *being itself*. In English that phrase, "being-itself," always sounds mystical in the derogatory sense. In Anglo-Saxon countries such as Great Britain and America, we have the greatest difficulty in conceiving of truth in any way that is not concrete, hard, and solid, or in terms which can not be reduced to something concrete, hard, and solid. We are so earth-bound!

Whereas Paulus cherished the mystical, he was keenly aware of its limitations. He writes:

The God above God is the object of all mystical longing, but mysticism must be transcended in order to reach him. Mysticism does not take seriously the concrete and the doubt concerning the concrete. It plunges directly into the ground of being and meaning, and leaves the concrete, the world of values and meanings, behind. Therefore it does not solve the problem of meaninglessness. In terms of the present religious situation this means that Eastern mysticism is not the solution of the problems of Western Existentialism, although many people attempt this solution.[11]

But every philosopher worthy of the name must have some way of leaping the gap when he has gone as far as his reason will take him. When he reached the limits of rationality, Plato used the myth. Someone else might express in a poem what Paulus is confronting in the last section of *The Courage to Be*. Paulus always presupposes the logos. Though this is the origin of logic, it is also partially a metaphor; and it connects him with the structure of meaning in the universe. I believe this logos serves for Paulus' leap.

Being-itself describes an encounter with reality below the subject-object split. That is the level where we have to seek reality, and with reality we find meaning. I cite my process of meditation as at least an analogy—at most a partial success—to the endeavor to make contact with being-itself. The process has something of the mystical, but it also has the techniques of psychoanalysis to keep it concrete. It has also my Protestant heritage to keep it aware of the social problems in our world of the market place.

At the point, however, where I touch and am aware of being-itself, there is something continually creative going on, something fascinating to watch and experience, something I cannot predict beforehand, something that often surprises me with its fecundity. It may say something very different from what I expect, and often amuses me greatly. It is a darkness, but a benign darkness, in which it is most pleasant to remain for a few

11. Tillich, op. cit., p. 186.

moments, and whose peace often stays with me during the
whole day. I am then frequently in the chaos of Genesis, surrounded by steam and vapor and unformed matter before the
worlds of night and day were created. But it is a benign chaos,
challenging me to take part in giving it form. It is limited only
by the limits of my imagination.

There are passages in Paulus' sermons which seem to have
this same thrust. I quote one:

> Nothing is demanded of you—no idea of God, and no goodness in
> yourselves, not your being religious, not your being Christian, not your
> being wise, and not your being moral. But what is demanded is only
> your being open and willing to accept what is given to you, the New
> Being, The Being of love and justice and truth, as it is manifest in Him
> Whose yoke is easy and Whose burden is light.[12]

Another section points out the errors in our Protestant over-
emphasis on moralism and rationalism. This passage makes the
desideratum *grace*, as in Christianity, and it is not unlike *Satori*
in Zen Buddhism:

> ... *You are accepted*, accepted by that which is greater than you, and
> the name of which you do not know. Do not ask for the name now;
> perhaps you will find it later. Do not try to do anything now; perhaps
> later you will do much. Do not seek for anything; do not perform
> anything; do not intend anything. *Simply accept the fact that you are
> accepted!* ... After such an experience we may not be better than
> before, and we may not believe more than before. But everything is
> transformed. In that moment, grace conquers sin, and reconciliation
> bridges the gulf of estrangement.[13]

4

Paulus' thought also meets another challenge facing human
beings in our day, man's relation to the cosmos. We are con-

---

12. *The Shaking of the Foundations* (New York: Charles Scribner's Sons,
1948), p. 102.
13. Ibid., p. 162.

fronting not only a new age but a style of life which has to be lived not merely in city or nation but in the universe. The practical effects of our trip to the moon may not have been very great. But symbolically it had infinite importance. The space voyage marked the first time since creation that men—men like you and me, with whom we identify—have seen the world from the perspective of space as a totality, one globe among other globes, one ball among an infinite number of other balls whirling in space.

Our religious task will be not only to move from the life-style of the city and nation to an internationalism on this particular globe, but to relate to the cosmos. As religion ideally should reach out ahead to the new tasks and challenges confronting us, it now points toward that new planetary dimension.

My faith and hope is that this new religious outlook will be characterized not only by internationalism but interracism and intersexism as well. I believe it will be an expansion for all of us: women (in their liberation), men (in *their* liberation, which will come unavoidably with that of women), and children (in their innocence, which can be preserved without imprisoning them in helplessness) I hope and believe that the new age will be a time when men and women can at last recognize each other as human, giving the respect and esteem to each other that human consciousness deserves.

Now Paul Tillich stands as the thinker who saw this cosmic relationship most clearly. Not only in his specific papers on space, though these are relevant. Not only in the concern of his method with man and culture. He saw it most significantly of all in his steadfast refusal to accept any beliefs that produce a theology of exclusion. This is the meaning of his statement quoted above, that there is demanded of us no belief in a particular God, nor of being religious in a particular sense, nor being Christian, nor being moral. The only thing demanded of us is that we accept what is given to us, the New Being.

CHAPTER 8

"Today Is
Dying Day"

Paulus and I used often to talk of death. He had none of the
feeling that it was an "untouchable" topic; there was no pornographic aura surrounding it in his mind. Death was an important, universal subject with which he was free and direct. Not
that he was not afraid of death; but he regarded it as complementary to life, interwoven with life. Death is the ultimate
symbol of our finiteness, of which weakness and illness are lesser
symbols.

Once, a few years before he himself died, he and I were
walking around his "park" as he was fond of calling it. This
consisted of the Tillich lawn, with many kinds of trees, which
in certain seasons of the year were incredibly rich in their
greenness, plus an adjacent plot of undeveloped land. Paulus
walked with his hands clasped behind him.

I said, "Paulus, are you afraid of dying?"

His face blanched slightly. "Yes. Everyone is. It's the Unknown. The great unknowable. Nobody has ever come back to
tell us."

No one knows. The Unknown. Such is the importance of
knowing, or more accurately of consciousness, for a man like

Paulus. No matter how often such a man thinks of suicide and reminds himself that it would "solve" a lot of problems and relieve a lot of heartaches, he still chooses to stay alive no matter what physical pain he has to bear so that he still can *know*, can see what goes on.

We talked more about the loneliness of death. I knew he did not believe in immortality in the pseudo-Christian sense in which it is bandied about in the West. He used often to say it had never been a Christian doctrine: it was Neoplatonic, bootlegged into Christianity. Ethically, it was selfish; psychologically, it was egocentric; economically it was an opiate for the masses as Karl Marx well said. The Christian doctrine, in contrast, is the resurrection—a very different thing.

When Paulus was depressed about the possibility of dying before he finished his systematic theology, I would reassure him with the comment that he would not die until his work was done. I meant that normally death requires a psychological and spiritual readiness as well as physical disintegration, and persons who are committed to a task seem to gain the energy necessary to keep on living until it is completed. Thus Kierkegaard wrote twenty books in fourteen years, completed them at the early age of forty-two, and then "in conclusion" took to his bed and died. Though it is dangerous to take this idea too literally, there is some truth in it. But the trouble with the case of Paulus came after the last volume of the systematics was completed, for I then was scared to death that he *would* die.

When he was in his late sixties, we had in New York a conference on death sponsored by the Association for Existential Psychology and Psychiatry. Gabriel Marcel was the featured speaker on the topic, "My Death and I." Paulus was the discussant and Paul Ricoeur was in the audience. Both Paulus and I had read copies of Marcel's paper. The night before, he and Hannah had taken me to see a play, and we discussed the paper afterward. Marcel's wife had died several years before, and in the paper he seemed to be trying to substantiate a conviction of hope which really came out of his understandable preoccupation with her death. Both Paulus and I thought it not up to his past standards.

The next day Gabriel Marcel delivered the speech to an overflow crowd. Everyone admired his spunk and honesty, despite his personal bias. In the following discussion Paul Ricoeur rose to speak (he had always said of Paulus, "He is *my* theologian" —exceptional praise from one so eminent as Ricoeur). Marcel had been one of Ricoeur's first teachers in philosophy, and it was fascinating to see these two distinguished French philosophers disagree in polite but impassioned old-world form. Ricoeur pointed out how personal hope could distort the topic, and that courage consisted of the capacity to face death without any mitigation of its starkness. The impassioned Marcel leaned forward, red-faced, and cried to Ricoeur, "What a great abyss separates us!"

In this discussion, Paulus stated that he would take the role of advocatus diaboli, the devil in this case being Heidegger. He outlined the concept that death is a necessary condition if life is to be understood; that life is complementary to death; that death is inevitable, and that an acceptance of it leads to greater capacity for joy in life. He repeated the phrase which was central in Heidegger: "Life is running forward toward death." It is a description of our existence.

Paulus himself surely did run forward toward death. His letters in his seventies tell of his increasing consciousness of death. In one to me on his seventy-fifth birthday he thanked me for my felicitations and added, "I enter my fourth quarter-century, in which death is certain to claim me."

Another letter to a beloved woman puts life in terms of warmth. He had returned from warm days in Washington, I assume in the spring, and recalls returning from the warm days in Athens several weeks earlier. He writes,

We need each other—others' warmth in a world which is colder than human nature demands—at least my nature. Give me your warmth. Don't stop giving it to me even if I am swallowed up by darkness, cold and silence.

Again he writes of the intermixture of life and death:

During the last weekend Life and Death came to me at the same day. We got René and Mary from the New London ferry as officially financés. . . . We are very happy, had a wonderful series of celebrations with them, Mutie and, one evening, the Mays. . . . Then Death came. My oldest friend, Hermann Schrafft died. . . . Every year of my life is full of memories concerning him. To me all this means more than I can express. I am much nearer death than I was in my feeling a few days ago. It is hard to anticipate non-being if one is bound with so many ties to being, e.g., flowers from our garden on my desk at which I am looking, the birds, the ocean, and those whom I love.

One letter consists of a sheet of paper with this written in the center in red pencil:

The last day
of a great and terrible year,
the year of our encounter and the year of death and sickness,
I am with you
I love you

Other letters tell of the increasing closeness of death:

Since the death of Hermann Schafft, death is very familiar to me. The feeling of the limited amount of years, this impenetrable wall, is always with me. . . .

. . . with innumerable official letters, preparation of my trip to Germany and more people here than Hannah's and my own weakness can stand. Beyond this: the house and park are beautiful, ocean as ever, but the strength is lacking. The day after tomorrow is my 76th birthday. . . .

There is a great love between us, perhaps too great for the limits of my heart and the slow decrease of my strength.

On October 12, 1965, I went to Lake Forest College, in a suburb of Chicago, to take part in a conference with Paulus and the students of the college on—of all subjects—death. There I learned that Paulus could not come and was indeed in the University Hospital. We all had premonitions that this illness (he being then seventy-nine) was "ultimate," if I may use one of his favorite words. His presence was felt even more strongly at the conference than if he had been there in person, for we knew he was dying. I phoned Hannah, but she said the doctor felt it would be better not to come down to see Paulus—another reason I felt the illness must be terminal.

I shall relate here what she later told me of his days during those last two weeks. He got progressively weaker. One day his voice began to rattle, and the doctor advised Hannah to call René and Mutie, telling them to come. The next morning she told Paulus they were coming, and he cried, "Oh, no, no! This is the end." He implored Hannah not to leave him all day long. But then he seemed to pull himself together.

"This is dying day," he said. A mood of sadness comes over me as I write about it now, but also hope and courage. For in his last day Paulus was still the creative teacher in that he showed how a human being may encounter his death.

He related to Hannah a dream he had had the night before in which a strange man addressed him in a nice voice, telling him someone was dying. "Is it René?" Paulus asked. The man nodded. Then someone else seemed to be dying. "Is it Hannah?" Paulus asked, and the answer again came in the affirmative. The dream seems to me to come out of his great loneliness on that final day. Such a dream also reflects the archetypal mode of meeting the loneliness by taking family members with one in death. This probably underlies the custom in such cultures as that of ancient Egypt of burying the dead man's wives and servants with him.

During that day Paulus went in and out of consciousness. He seemed to go into death, across some River Styx, and was with old friends who had died: Kurt Goldstein, and probably Hermann Schafft. He said, "I cannot differentiate myself from others. I do not know where I leave off and other personalities begin." Then his consciousness would come back to earth. It was the strange experience of a man going in and out of death, almost at will. It bespeaks the land of the partially dead, as the ancient Greeks saw it.

He spoke of the river of time. "It flows in a straight line," he said, "on into infinity. But it is now empty of content."

When the doctor came in about noon, Paulus joked with him. "Today I'm going to be a complete ascetic. I spent a long time yesterday figuring out the menu for today, but I'm not going to eat a thing."

The doctor laughed outright. "That's the first time I ever heard it put that way."

During the afternoon he wanted Hannah to bring him his books. He asked Hannah's forgiveness for what he had done that pained her, which she readily gave. Then he recalled that they would never again walk around their "park" together. At this he began to cry. Hannah assured him that she would remember him as she walked in the park. They recited together a little German poem they used to say together on their walks.

About seven in the evening he told the nurse and Hannah that he wanted to get up and walk. The nurse helped him sit up and dangle his legs over the edge of the bed. Then he lay back down and died.

There is another dying day which always comes into my mind whenever I think of Paulus. Socrates also joked on the day he died. Despite its obvious dissimilarities, Paulus' dying day has some resemblance to that described at the end of *Phaedo*.

... he raised the cup to his lips, and showing not the least distaste, quite unperturbed, he drained the draught. Most of us had till then been

more or less able to restrain our tears, but when we saw him drinking
and then that he had drunk it, we could do so no longer. For my part,
despite my efforts I found that tears flooded down my cheeks; I
wrapped my face in my cloak and wept for my misfortune—not for his,
but for my own, to think what I friend I had lost. . . .

When the poison reaches the heart, [said Socrates], that will be the
end. He was beginning to grow cold about the groin, when he uncovered his face, for he had covered himself up, and said: Crito, I owe a
cock to Asclepius; will you remember to pay the debt?

The debt shall be paid, said Crito; is there anything else? There was
no answer to this question; but in a minute or two a movement was
heard, and the attendants covered him; his eyes were set, and Crito
closed his eyes and mouth.

Such was the end, Echecrates, of our Friend; concerning whom I
may say, that of all the men of his time whom I have known, he was
the wisest and the justest and the best.

Eight months after Paulus was cremated, the jar containing
his ashes was disinterred in East Hampton, where it had been
buried, and brought to New Harmony, Indiana, where the Paul
Tillich Park is located. This little town is a monument to two
utopias, the first that of the Raffites, a religious community from
central Europe, followed ten years later by the socialists under
Robert Owen. These utopias were practical failures, but aes-
thetically they were a remarkable success: there remains a community of houses a century and a half old, each of which is a
museum piece. Here Paulus had come, at the invitation of his
friend Jane Owen, who had purchased most of the houses, to
accept dedication of the park in his name. Mrs. Owen invited
him to select the trees he would like to have in it. Those he
picked were of course mainly trees from Germany which he
had loved as a boy, and the slips were duly ordered and shipped
across the sea to the park. The German fir trees had grown
roughly to the height of my shoulder when his ashes were in-
terred in an opening among them. On rocks throughout the
place are carved verses from Paulus' writings, and his head,
sculptured and cast in bronze by Rosatti, stands on a pedestal

among the trees. It is fitting, since he began life among those trees in a village in eastern Germany, that his ashes now lie among the same trees in a village in midwestern America.

A memorial service was held at Pentecost in 1966 in the roofless church adjacent to the park. I venture to conclude this small volume with the address which I gave on that occasion, which contains as true a summary of Tillich's meaning to us all as I am capable of setting down.

In this lovely place in the month of May, I find my mind filled with memories of an experience in May four years ago, which gave me an unforgettable picture of our friend whose life we celebrate today. It was in the Busch-Reisinger Museum in Cambridge. A dinner was being given to honor Paul Tillich on the occasion of his retirement from his university professorship at Harvard. During the dinner a string quartet played Bach from the balcony. All around the walls of the museum were old German wood sculptures, large medieval and Gothic forms that had been carved by the hands of Germans before the time of Jacob Boehme. These old figures in their rich dark brown and gray wood were the most fitting surroundings for the event, for they spoke silently and eloquently of the eternal polarities in Paul Tillich—the daimonic and the beautiful, the tragic and the joyful, the everlasting forms and the transitory reminders of one's homeland.

Late in the evening, after the other speeches, Paul Tillich arose to give his response. He spoke two or three sentences in his moving and measured way which we all remember. Suddenly there was a clap of thunder, and a terrific spring rainstorm broke loose. The rain came down so hard on the roof above us that the lights went out and the next two sentences of Tillich's speech were drowned out. Then in a momentary lull we heard Tillich's calm sentences going steadily on. Again came a clap of thunder and the windows lighted up with lightning and the

*very earth on which the museum stood seemed to shake. Transfi-
gured there, the figure with the large head and white hair spoke
calmly, unruffled, as though he were right in his element in this
Wagnerian upheaval of the skies—as indeed he was. The spring
cloudburst continued for the full half hour Tillich spoke, a
wonderful and awe-inspiring antiphony of nature with a remarkable man.*

*What was so amazingly gripping was that nature itself
seemed to surround Paul Tillich and confirm him with exactly
the daimonic and the earth-bound elements from the depths of
the universe which were the sources of his own deepest thoughts
and feelings. We saw and heard a man speaking with the tremendous power of his logic, a man bringing the logos into
human life by his philosophy and theology, a man great in the
transcendent dimensions of his mind and spirit—but a man
who was part of the storm, who stood at the same moment with
his feet on the earth there in the mud and in the grass which
gets wet with the spring rain. And it seemed that nature, knowing this, joined in the musical antiphony, and affirmed that
there was a man who was a great thinker, one who could live
in eternal essences, but at the same time a man standing with
his feet in the grass and the mud and the rain of our everyday
earth.*

*And now, on Pentecost, we gather to pay homage to the life
he lived with us, and to meditate on the meaning of that life.
Let us take the distinguishing mark of Pentecost, "speaking in
tongues," as Tillich's capacity to speak the language of the
many diverse groups in our culture. One of the special values
of his work was that his influence was not at all confined to
theology and philosophy, but was present in art, in education
from the smallest college to the greatest university, in politics,
and in psychiatry and psychotherapy. Many of us feel a poig-
nant pride that we can be part of these movements in our
culture of which he was so often the most profound interpreter.*

But the wonderful thing about Paul Tillich was that he never made disciples of us, nor did he ever attract mere followers. His whole life was an embodiment of Nietzsche's clarion call, "Follow not me but yourself." He made us all colleagues, co-workers, and co-creaters.

I ask, with respect to my own field of psychoanalysis, what was the special contribution Paul Tillich made? From all over the country came the same reports, that whenever he spoke the psychologists, psychiatrists, and psychoanalysts came out in large numbers to hear him. They listened with rapt attention. What were they listening for? To hear a great mind in action? There are other great minds—minds of wisdom and erudition —and to these they do not listen with the same raptness.

The first answer to our question of his amazingly wide influence is that Tillich spoke out of our broken culture, but he spoke believing. Others have spoken out of our broken culture, but with defiance, not affirmation. Others have spoken with belief, but from an ethereal philosophical or religious height outside our human culture, which leaves us cold, for we psychoanalysts must stand upon the earth, no matter how slimy or muddy or fog-bound it may be.

But believing is caring. The most significant motive in the coming of these psychiatrists and psychologists to Tillich was their yearning for help in the capacity to cure. In these professions, which must remain related to science and the earthbound aspects of man or they are lost, it is difficult to sustain "belief-ful realism," to use a phrase from one of Tillich's earliest books. In the professions which deal intimately with the human soul, it is easy to become despairing. If we take seriously what we are dealing with—intimate suffering and conflict, which often racks the human psyche and is portentous for meaningful integration or dissolution of the self—we either believe strongly or we are bound to become cynical. Here the psychotherapist is in a position parallel to that of the minister, if the minister takes his priesthood seriously and does not evade his despair by the usual defense, "God does the work through me." The psychoanalyst is likewise tempted to evade his despair by the rubric, "Science does it through me." One hopes that God does work through the priest and science through the therapist. But if these are used as defenses against despair, the therapist's presence will not be there, his technique will become hollow, and he will find himself unable to empathize with the patient or participate in the meaning the patient gives to his struggles. Paul Tillich gave us the capacity to believe even though honest men differ in the content of beliefs. He taught us the importance of ultimate concern.

Another great contribution he made was his emphasis upon and elaboration of the meaningfulness of the daimonic. We psychiatrists and psychologists live and work with the same daimonic; we invite the daimonic. And if you live and work on that level without believing strongly, you become part of the daimonic system. Tillich not only recognizes the daimonic with which we must deal, but he makes it an integral part of his philosophy. He not only stands within our anxiety, guilt, and despair, but he points out that these are an inescapable part of man's life as man. We thus do not need to be guilty about despair, nor anxious about our guilt. The daimonic then need not develop into "demon possession," but may become the source and impetus of human creativity.

But I do not think it is for relief of guilt that my professional colleagues and other intellectuals read Tillich. Rather it is for the sense of having our feet on the bedrock of existence by recognizing the inevitability of anxiety, despair, and guilt in the human situation, which is the first step in helping ourselves and our patients to have the "courage to be." It is a great relief to find that our science does not have to carry the burden of perfection, nor do we have to either. I think our work with the people we seek to help is then interfused with a quality of

deeper understanding and mercy—and if I may use this term
without hubris, a quality of grace. It seems to me, thus, that
Tillich is the therapist for the therapists.

There is another reason why our gathering here today has a
special significance. This is illustrated by an ancient myth, the
death of Oedipus in the last pages of Sophocles' play, Oedipus
in Colonus. *I have often meditated during these last months on*
that drama as I have thought about the life and death of
Paulus.

It was believed in Thebes and Athens that a special peace
would come to the nation which possessed the body of old
Oedipus after his death, and that Oedipus himself had,
through having come to terms with his tragic experiences
through his sufferings, a special power to impart grace. As he
says to the natives who find him with his daughter in the grove
at Colonus:

> For I come here as one endowed with grace,
> By those who are over Nature; and I bring
> Advantage to this race. . . .

Theseus accepts this: "Your presence, as you say, is a great
blessing."

In like manner, in our ceremony today, we have the hope and
belief that there is a grace imparted by Paulus. The symbol of
his ashes means that to all of us who have known him, to the
thousands who have read him, and to the tens of thousands who
have heard of him.

Old Oedipus' death is described with touching poignancy:

> But some attendant from the train of Heaven
> Came for him; or else the underworld
> Opened in love the unlit door of earth.
> For he was taken without lamentation,
> Illness or suffering; indeed his end
> Was wonderful if mortal's ever was.

In Sophocles' drama there is one thing about Oedipus' death which becomes transcendent in importance even over grace. This is love. The messenger who came back to the people to report the marvelous manner of Oedipus' death states that his last communication to his daughter was:

> . . . And yet one word
> Frees us of all the weight and pain of life:
> That word is love.

In these past months we have heard much about Paul Tillich's fame as a theologian and thinker. But great as his work was, there is one simple but profound thing of greater importance to us. This is that he loved us and we loved him.

He believed that love was creative, and for him it surely was. We knew him as a man of eros, philia, *and* agape. *One of the sources of his great power was that all three dimensions of love were present in what he felt and thought and did. He was always ready to respond with vitality; he never seemed to be depleted; he gave so much, but he also drew so much from the love of his friends. We were gripped in the deepest parts of our hearts by the powerful encounters with him, which shook us and searched us with an intensity which called forth our own most profound emotions.*

I have said that one of the things that contributed to Paul Tillich's vast influence was that he spoke out of our broken culture but he always spoke believing. The same was true of his love. He loved out of a broken society, and he knew only too well the tragedies and suffering, the daimonic and evil aspects of human love. But he loved believing.

Many of us who worked with him had never understood what the Biblical expression meant, "The Lord chastiseth whom he loveth," until we knew Paulus. When he was our advisor, in our various researches and study, more than one of us complained to him that he drove us too hard. He would answer only with his gentle but inexorable smile; his love to us was relentless in his calm insistence on our best. It was a magnificent grace to us that he would not let us escape from becoming what we truly are.

I close with some sentences from Paul Tillich's own hand in a letter he wrote to a friend after the death of a mutual friend. These express better than I can the deep meaning of this moment for us today. "I am fully convinced," Paul wrote, "of the dimension of the eternal in a human being. In the light of the eternal I do not see him [our friend who died] or myself in isolation. The individual destiny ceases to be individual alone in that which lies beyond temporal existence and for which we only have poor symbols."

He concludes his letter, "We are given existence in time. The meaning of it is that we shall give meaning to these transistory hours in creation, joy, love, power. All this has an eternal dimension and a transitory, but it is not only transitory, and therefore is it worthy to be lived—in spite of."

This Paul Tillich certainly achieved. His love and joy and power are procreative in all of us. And I am convinced that this creation will continue, for our later world will desperately need his ultimate concern.

73 74 75 76 77 10 9 8 7 6 5 4 3 2 1